THE

United States Political System

AND HOW IT WORKS

by
DAVID CUSHMAN COYLE

A SIGNET KEY BOOK
Published by THE NEW AMERICAN LIBRARY

COPYRIGHT, 1954, BY DAVID CUSHMAN COYLE

All rights reserved

Published as a SIGNET KEY BOOK

FIRST PRINTING, FEBRUARY, 1954

Library of Congress Catalog Card No. 54-6829

*SIGNET KEY BOOKS are published by
The New American Library of World Literature, Inc.
501 Madison Avenue, New York 22, New York*

PRINTED IN THE UNITED STATES OF AMERICA

The Mechanics of Democracy

"Politics is the way the human race behaves when it has democracy. In a democratic society, conflicting opinions on the government's acts and policies are ordinarily worked out without getting into a civil war. By politics the people provide the standards of judgment, and choose the government officials to apply them, so as to get a result that will not be intolerable to any important part of the community."

"American politics, good and bad, expresses the mixed character of the American people, and the past history in which not only governmental institutions but political habits have taken shape . . ."

DAVID CUSHMAN COYLE

This is a lively, challenging exposition of the United States political system and the complex network of organizations and agencies that make it work day by day and state by state. An invaluable key to understanding the intricate mechanics of U.S. democracy. This volume also explains the philosophy which makes the operation work.

MENTOR Books of Special Interest
Only 35 cents each

A DOCUMENTARY HISTORY OF THE UNITED STATES
by Richard D. Heffner
A unique collection—35 important documents that have shaped America's history, never before assembled in a single low-cost volume. With a commentary showing their significance. (#M78)

THE LIVING U. S. CONSTITUTION
edited by Saul K. Padover
The complete text of one of the world's greatest documents, the basis of American democracy; the story of its making and the men who framed it, important Supreme Court decisions affecting its interpretation, and a comprehensive index. (#M95)

AMERICAN DIPLOMACY: 1900-1950 *by George F. Kennan*
A trenchant appraisal of United States' foreign relations during the last fifty years by a distinguished diplomat. (#M80)

THE AGE OF JACKSON (abridged)
by Arthur M. Schlesinger, Jr.
The Pulitzer Prize winning story of the Jackson era, and the struggle which produced a great philosophy of equity, justice and opportunity. (#M38)

JEFFERSON (revised and abridged) *by Saul K. Padover*
One of the best biographies of a great American statesman, the third President of the United States, this stirring book shows Jefferson as farmer, philosopher, and architect of freedom and democracy. (#M70)

TO OUR READERS

We welcome your comments about SIGNET or MENTOR Books, as well as your suggestions for new reprints. If your dealer does not have the books you want, you may order them by mail, enclosing the list price plus 5c a copy to cover mailing costs. Send for a copy of our complete catalog. The New American Library of World Literature, Inc., 501 Madison Ave., New York 22, New York.

Table of Contents

Chapter		Page
I:	*Origins*	7
II:	*The Parties*	19
III:	*Party Organization and Operation*	33
IV:	*The Administration*	46
V:	*Congress—What Is It?*	56
VI:	*Congress at Work*	64
VII:	*Federal Courts*	73
VIII:	*The States*	82
IX:	*Local Government*	93
X:	*Government and Business*	99
XI:	*Individual Rights*	106
XII:	*The American Philosophy of Government*	118
XIII:	*Foreign Relations*	130
XIV:	*Politics and Democracy*	142
	Index	149

I.

ORIGINS

POLITICS IS THE WAY THE HUMAN RACE BEHAVES WHEN IT has democracy. In a democratic society, conflicting opinions on the government's acts and policies are ordinarily worked out without getting into a civil war. By politics the people provide the standards of judgment and choose the government officials to apply them so as to get a result that will not be intolerable to any important part of the community.

American politics, good and bad, expresses the mixed character of the American people and the past history in which not only governmental institutions but political habits have taken shape. The American form of government is partly an inheritance from the British colonial system of the 1700's and partly a new invention designed to meet the peculiar circumstances of American history.

Today only about half the American people are of British blood; nearly all the others are Continental Europeans, Negroes, or American Indians. There are a few Orientals. The political system by which the Americans operate their government is a product more of instinct than of logical planning. It is based mainly on British customs and traditions, but includes contributions from all the kinds of people that inhabit the United States. This book is intended to show how political parties and political activities operate upon the various agencies of government in this country.

In the British American colonies during the Colonial period from 1607 to 1776, the English forms of government were established that would later be the foundation of most of the present political institutions of the country.

The Colonial legislatures made laws for the Colonies, chartered local governments, levied taxes, and made appropriations for public expenses. They sometimes used the power of the purse to control the actions of the governor.

Local governments were modeled after those in England. According to local circumstances the Colonies had counties, townships, manors, and boroughs, many of which continue to this day with little fundamental change. County courts and justices of the peace, sheriffs and coroners, were all familiar to the Colonists before the Revolution. There were intermediate courts in each colony to try serious cases, and supreme courts to hear appeals. The final appeal was to the Privy Council in England.

The colonists took for granted the traditional rights of Englishmen, such as the right of meeting and petitioning the Government, the right of jury trial, and the right to elect representatives to the legislature that levied the taxes. During most of the Colonial period the colonists paid no taxes to England—and got no military aid from England, although the British Government repeatedly thrust them into wars against the French and the French Indians of Canada. When the British Parliament finally attempted to tax the Americans, who had no representation in Westminster, the Americans regarded the tax as a violation of their ancestral rights.

Because of the great distance and slow communications across the Atlantic Ocean, the Colonial governments had more freedom than the strict letter of the law was supposed to give them. Especially in their local governments and along the slowly advancing frontier, the Americans saw few signs of their lord the king. They became used to a large measure of self-government and self-reliance during their hundred and seventy years under the British flag. But the fact that their governmental system headed up in the person of the king and in a Parliament where they had no representation, prevented any such growth of organized political parties as occurred after the Colonies broke with England. The chief political controversies were between the governors and the legislatures or between candidates for local office.

During the Colonial period there were several proposals for setting up a Colonial union of some kind to manage the frequent wars with the French and Indains. These plans were never carried through, but the idea of united action became familiar to the Americans. When the disputes with England grew more and more bitter in the early 1770's, the Americans took up seriously the idea of united action. In 1774 they called a Continental Congress.

The Continental Congress had no legal basis: it was merely an unofficial indignation meeting. It passed a Declaration of Rights and Grievances and called another Congress for 1775. This Congress took more definite shape, in response to the fact that the shooting war had begun in Massachusetts. It assumed the right to govern the Colonies. It raised a national army and appointed George Washington to be its Commander in Chief.

The Second Continental Congress voted the Declaration of Independence in 1776. The Declaration asserted the traditional rights of Englishmen and the inalienable rights of free men as the foundation on which the American States based their claim to set up a government of their own. The Declaration of Independence has no force of law like the Constitution, but it has great authority as a statement of the moral principles by which political actions can be judged in the United States.

In 1777 the Continental Congress adopted a proposal for a loose federal union and sent it to the States to be ratified. All the States had ratified by 1781, and the document, known as the Articles of Confederation, became the first constitution of the Republic.

The Federal Government set up by the Articles of Confederation was too simple and too weak to be practical, but it was all that the States would accept at the time. The few powers that the States were willing to grant to the Government were entrusted to Congress, a single assembly in which each State had one vote. There was no executive branch, and no judiciary.

Under the Articles of Confederation the nation and the States slid rapidly toward disaster. The Continental money inflated until it was practically worthless, so that to this day the phrase "not worth a continental" is a part of the American language. Trade between the States fell to a desperately low ebb. Many American businessmen began to call for a stronger Federal Government that could regulate commerce, levy taxes, and stop the collapse of the economic system. There were two interstate conferences of businessmen, in 1785 and 1786, which led to the calling of the Convention at Philadelphia in 1787, where the Constitution was written. The Constitution was therefore built around the "commerce clause" and the companion clauses giving the Federal Government various economic powers and duties.

These clauses represented the principal purpose of the men who brought about the Convention and of the men who attended it.

Most of the delegates to the Philadelphia Convention were lawyers, landowners, or businessmen who had served in Congress or as public officials. There were no representatives of the wage earners or small farmers, or of the pioneers along the frontier. The delegates wanted to make a government that would help business and that would be strong and enduring. They wanted a government responsible to the "people," but they had no intention of allowing the mass of the people to elect the President or even the Congress. And they had to find some compromise between the large and small States that would overcome their mutual jealousies and fears.

Federalism was a necessary feature of the Constitution, since it was intended to create a strong central government and at the same time to let the States keep all the powers that did not absolutely have to be transferred to the nation. Behind this double purpose was the fear of tyranny in case the Federal Government were to become too strong. The same fear lay back of the doctrine of separation of powers —the idea that the legislative, executive, and judicial features of government might become dangerous if all three, or any two of them, should be concentrated in the same hands.

In view of the fact that the Constitution of the United States has endured without successful challenge since 1788, there can be no question that in the main it has suited the needs and the temperament of the American people. The men who wrote it had an amazing understanding of the American character and of the lessons of history drawn from other times and places. The result of their labors was remarkable not only for solving the immediate problems of 1788 but also for adjusting itself to circumstances which the founders could not have foreseen.

A century later the distinguished British observer, James Bryce, wrote of the United States Constitution:

"It ranks above every other written constitution for the intrinsic excellence of its scheme, its adaptation to the circumstances of the people, the simplicity, brevity and precision of its language, its judicious mixture of definiteness in principle with elasticity in details." [1]

The Federal Government, created by the Constitution, was a synthetic sovereign State, in much the same way that a corporation is a synthetic person, or an electronic brain is a synthetic thinking machine. It was made, not born; the living flesh that now covers its bones has been added by the men who have made it work—that is, by Americans practicing the arts of politics and sometimes of statesmanship.

The States were the natural-born sovereigns. They had won in the war the power to exercise in their own territory all the sovereign rights of free Englishmen and from there on to define their sovereignty subject only to the law of nations.

When the Revolutionary War began, the States set up informal legislatures, and between 1776 and 1780 they adopted constitutions and created fully organized governments. Many of the principles that later went to form the Federal structure were previously tried by one or more of the States. The first State constitutions were short, but they were intended to be complete. For example, the States had separate legislative, executive, and judicial branches, which the Federal Government under the Articles of Confederation did not.

Under the Articles of Confederation, the principle was established that each State was a free and independent sovereign in its own right and that the United States had no powers except those given to it, or "delegated," by the States. When the new constitution came to be written, it had to be constructed on the same principle, with the difference that the new union would be "more perfect," that is, would have more delegated powers.

When the delegates came together at Philadelphia in 1787 they were authorized only to meet and propose amendments to the Articles of Confederation. The Articles provided that amendments could be adopted only by unani-

[1] James Bryce, *The American Commonwealth* (New York, The Macmillan Company, 1889), I, 25.

mous vote of the States. But when the delegates got down to work they found that nothing less than a completely new government would serve. They decided to scrap not only the Articles of Confederation but also the amending clause that offered a legal method for changing the basic law. Instead, they wrote into the new constitution its own adoption clause, establishing a new union of the first nine States to ratify. The others could come in when they got ready.

The principal work of the Convention consisted of designing a government that could carry the responsibilities which the delegates wanted to lay upon it and at the same time meet the objections that stood in the way of its adoption. Americans view the present-day efforts to unite the States of Western Europe with a sympathy based on historic experience. They have learned as children in school how the founders struggled with much the same problems.

When the Convention met it was presented with a detailed set of proposals, representing the interests of the larger States, which came to be known as the "Virginia Plan." In opposition the smaller states drew up a different scheme, which was called the "New Jersey Plan." The debate raged around the choice between these rival plans.

The two plans had some points in common, such as, for instance, the separation of powers. They both provided for separate legislative, executive, and judicial branches of the Government. But the point of conflict that created the most difficult problem was the form of the legislature and its relation to the power of the large and small States. This conflict threatened to disrupt the Convention. It was a problem that in our own time has arisen again in the Charter of the United Nations; and it must always trouble any combination of large and small states that proposes to act on controversial issues.

The Virginia Plan, following the familiar pattern of Colonial government with its upper and lower houses, proposed a congress of two chambers. One chamber was to be made up of members elected by the people, and they in turn would elect the members of the upper chamber from candidates nominated by the State legislatures. The main point of controversy was that in both chambers the States would be represented in proportion to their population or their taxes or some combination of the two. This arrangement would have given the larger States the full advantage of their size, which they did not have in the Continental Congress, where each State had one vote.

The New Jersey Plan called for a much less drastic change from the existing government. The plan proposed a congress of only one chamber, in which the States would each have one vote, just as under the Articles.

For many weeks the delegates argued over this difficult problem. How could large and small States belong to the same government with a fair division of power? Since there is no perfect answer to such a question, the argument threw doubt on whether a workable united government could be created.

Finally William Samuel Johnston of Connecticut offered the solution, which came to be known as the "Connecticut Compromise." There would be a House of Representatives, in which the States would be represented in proportion to population, and which would have the exclusive right to originate all bills for raising money. There would also be an upper house in which the States would have equal representation. This plan was adopted.

Since, in order to become law, a bill must pass both the House of Representatives and the Senate, in effect the small States can block a bill that hurts their interests by joining to vote against it in the Senate; and the larger States similarly can block a bill by their more numerous votes in the House. The system works so well, indeed, that the conflict of interest between large and small States, which loomed so dark on the horizon in 1787, has not turned out to be so common a cause of trouble as the founders thought it would be. Geographical conflicts of interest are more apt to be sectional or to represent the different interests of industrial, agricultural, and mining areas.

For example, New Mexico and Arizona are much smaller in population than California, and those States have been in a long dispute over the division of the Colorado River waters impounded by the Hoover Dam. But the larger States and the smaller States have not lined up in Congress to settle this dispute on a basis of their size.

The Constitution provided that members of the lower house were to be elected by the people—that is, by those who had the vote. The States reserved the right to restrict the suffrage to free white men with certain property and religious qualifications.

In his *History of the American People,* Woodrow Wilson estimates that in the early days, out of about 4,000,000 inhabitants, 120,000 had the right to vote.

Even that system was considered almost dangerously democratic in the eighteenth century. During the next hundred years the right to vote was given to more and more kinds of people. The frontier moved rapidly westward, and as new States were formed, the influence of the frontiersmen pushed the country toward equality. By 1860 practically all the States allowed the vote to all white men over twenty-one years old. After the Civil War, the Constitution was amended to give the vote to Negro men, although some of the Southern States have succeeded in throwing numerous obstacles in the way of Negro voting. The suffrage was given to women by an amendment to the Constitution in 1920.

The Senate was intended to be further removed from the people than the House. The Constitution therefore provided that the two senators from each State should be elected by the State legislatures. The effect was that the Senate was generally more conservative than the House. The senators were often rich men or men in close sympathy with large business and banking interests. The pressure toward a more inclusive democracy, sparked by political interests opposed to the conservatives, finally brought about an amendment in 1913 giving the people of the States the right to elect their senators directly.

Since 1913 the senators, instead of being kind of ambassadors or delegates sent to Washington to represent the governments of their States, are more nearly like congressmen raised to a larger size.

In recent years the Senate has often been less conservative than the House. Many observers have felt that the House leans on the Senate to reject the unwise and reckless measures that House members vote for under pressure from powerful influences. When the voters are impatient and wrong-headed, the Senate will often stand up against popular clamor, relying on a change of sentiment. The senators have rather more independence, since they serve six-year terms, while the Representatives must face the voters every two years. The House often cuts appropriations for government services below a practical level so as to make a record of "economy." But the congressmen rely on the senators to restore what funds are necessary to operate the Government.

The Constitution originally provided that the President should be elected by the electoral college, a group of distinguished men from each State, chosen in any way that the State might prefer—by the legislature, the people, or even the governor. There was no intention of letting the people elect the President or even choose the electors unless their State so decided.

Here the pressure for democracy has quietly changed the meaning of the Constitution without bothering to pass a corresponding amendment. Each political party puts up candidates for elector, all of them pledged to vote for their party candidates for President and Vice-President. The electors have no free choice, and party hacks of no distinguished qualifications for choosing a President are often flattered by being made electors.

In 1948 there was a threat that the customary system would be ruined by some electors in the Southern States running as Democrats and then voting against Mr. Truman, the Democratic candidate. Mr. Truman was elected, but the dangers of public confusion and possible frustration of the will of the people were brought to public attention.

Another feature of the electoral college, not provided in the Constitution, is the custom in every State of giving all the electoral votes to the party that wins the State. The losing party, even if it gets 49 per cent of the popular vote, gets no electors. The effect is to make the national electoral vote vastly different from the national popular vote. The winner may get 55 per cent of the voters but his electoral vote may be 80 or 90 per cent. Such a result gives an appearance of "making it unanimous" that may help to give authority to the voice of the President, especially in world affairs.

But it also brings in the possibility that one candidate may get a popular majority, concentrated in a few States, while the other, by barely squeaking through in the States with the majority of electoral votes, may win the Presidency. In 1888, for instance, Grover Cleveland got a majority of the people's votes, but Benjamin Harrison was elected President. This possibility is generally held to be a bad feature of the system, although it does cut down the relative importance of the "one-party" States. The question might be raised whether a State that does not engage in two-party political controversy on a vigorous scale should have as large a part in the choice of a President as one that can boast a healthy two-party system.

American opinion seems to favor the substitution of some more logical method that will be sure to give effect to the popular majority and that will avoid the danger of an elector suddenly digging up his Constitutional right and voting to suit his own ideas. But there is also a vast lethargy about passing any of the proposed amendments, so long as no spectacular frustration of the popular will occurs.

The Constitution was carefully designed to provide a "system of checks and balances," to prevent any branch of the government running amok.

The President, for instance, may veto an act of Congress. The act then goes back to Congress and cannot become law unless both houses pass it again by a two-thirds vote.

The Congress can veto many kinds of Presidential action, including the use of his Constitutional powers as Commander in Chief, by refusing to provide the money.

The Senate can veto a treaty negotiated by the President. All the important officials of the Administration and all Federal judges are appointed by the President, subject to the consent of the Senate.

The Constitution failed to provide that the Supreme Court could nullify acts of Congress as unconstitutional, but the logic of events has allowed the Court to assume that power.

The President, the members of the Supreme Court, and all other important officials of the executive and judicial branches can be removed from office by impeachment. In an impeachment proceeding the House prosecutes and the Senate sits as a court. President Johnson escaped impeachment by a margin of one vote in the Senate. The Senate has voted for impeachment in only four cases, all involving Federal judges.

The principle of checks and balances contradicts the principle of separation of powers, and the two together represent the kind of practical compromise that so often appeals to the American mind. It is impossible to get the legislative, executive, and judicial powers absolutely separated, yet it is desirable to keep any two of them from getting into the hands of one would-be dictator or of one secret-police system. The partial separation and the checks and balances were designed to protect the country against what we now call "totalitarianism"; and so far they have succeeded.

The men who wrote the Constitution did not provide a general "bill of rights" to protect the citizens against oppressive acts of the Federal Government. Here and there, to be sure, were clauses forbidding certain wrongs that had been suffered in the past at the hands of the king and Parliament. In Article I the Government was forbidden to pass a bill of attainder, by which an individual and his family could be singled out for punishment. It was forbidden to pass any *ex post facto* law, a law making an action a crime which had not been a crime when it was done.

The right of habeas corpus was guaranteed, to protect the people from arbitrary imprisonment by the police, such as we have seen in many totalitarian countries. In Article III the trial of Federal crime is required to be by jury. The charge of treason, often used by kings in those days for what the communists now call "purging," was carefully protected from abuse.

But when the Constitution was submitted to the States to be ratified, the opposition criticized it for not including a complete bill of rights. Some of the States gave their ratification with the understanding that one of the first acts of the new Congress would be to start the amendment process for adding such a bill to the Constitution.

The Bill of Rights, consisting of the first ten amendments, differs in many details from the Declaration of Human Rights adopted by the United Nations Assembly. The types of wrong that Englishmen of the late 1700's had suffered from their government or that their ancestors had abolished after long and bitter struggle were the background for the rights guaranteed to the Americans by their Constitution. But in our own day other wrongs have been invented or revived from ancient and savage times by Hitler and the Soviets. The principle is still the same.

These were the principal features of the Constitution. They have provided a stout framework on which the political forces of the American people could build whatever the sovereign people decided to build. Some, such as the election and powers of the Congress, have come down to the present day with little fundamental change. Others, such as the powers of the electoral college and those of the Supreme Court, have been transformed. But the Constitution as a whole has continued to do the work for which it was originally designed—to provide a government strong enough to act for the American people as a nation, while at the same time maintaining its subservience to the American people as a sovereign.

I I.

THE PARTIES

THE AMERICAN PEOPLE PLAINLY WANT A TWO-PARTY system. During the past two hundred years, whenever they have found themselves with only one party, they have split it in two or started a new one. When they have found themselves faced with three parties they have killed one at the polls.

In the Colonial period the Whigs and Tories represented widely different political attitudes—so wide, in fact, that in 1775 their conflict led to war. At present, the two parties are more nearly alike; they are sometimes called Tweedledum and Tweedledee. Every two years they agree to have a battle in which both sides are well enough protected to avoid serious damage to the loser.

The peculiarities of the American parties are the result of the country's history and circumstances rather than of anything planned by the political leaders. In fact one of the most striking features of the Constitution is that it does not mention parties.

Before the Revolution there were no parties organized in modern form. But some people, who were usually on the side of the king and the royal governors, were called Tories; and others, who were apt to favor the Colonial legislatures and the principles of self-government, were often called Whigs. The conflict between Whigs and Tories was settled by the war. The Whigs, or "Patriots," not only won the war; they completely eliminated the opposition. The Tories were driven out and fled to Canada or the Bahamas.

Although conservatives in the United States today are sometimes called Tories, there has never been any party in this country trying to restore the king of England since the Revolution.

The United States, therefore, like all revolutionary countries, began as a one-party political system. George Washington and many others among the Revolutionary leaders wanted it to stay that way. Washington in his Farewell Address warned the people earnestly against parties, "with particular reference to the founding of them on geographical discriminations." He also warned "in the most solemn manner against the baleful effects of the spirit of party generally. . . ." It "foments occasionally riot and insurrection."

Washington remembered the bitter war between Whigs and Tories. He foresaw the situation that might arise if parties were concentrated in different parts of the country, where they could set up rival governments and raise armies, as in fact they did afterwards in 1861.

James Madison, arguing for the adoption of the Constitution in the Federalist Papers, took pains to point out that the new Federal Government had the advantage of being designed "to break and control the violence of faction."

The electoral college, for instance, was particularly designed to avoid party politics in the choice of the President. Many of the founders thought of the President as a sort of elected king, who would stand above parties like the present-day President of France or King of England. The Constitution in its original form directed that the electors in each state were to meet and each to vote for two persons, without stating any preference. Then the man getting the most votes would be President and the runner-up would be Vice-President. This system was thought to be a guarantee that the best and second-best men, according to the opinion of the leading people, would always be chosen as President and Vice-President.

Even in 1787, when the Constitution was written, the people were divided over whether to ratify it, although they were not yet organized into definite political parties. In general the merchants, bankers, and conservative landowners, led by Alexander Hamilton, wanted the Constitution. The workers and farmers, and especially the local politicians, fearing the loss of state and local self-government, opposed it. The Constitution was adopted by a slim margin, and only because the right to vote was limited to a small percentage of the population, mainly those with property.

But the popularity of George Washington and the good

effects of the Constitution on trade and prosperity prevented the organization of opposing parties until near the end of Washington's second term. Then the question of who should be the new President began to divide the people into political organizations backing opposing candidates. On one side were the Federalists, representing business, finance, and the middle classes of city folk; and strongest in the Northeastern States. On the other were the "Republicans" led by Thomas Jefferson. They represented mainly the country folk, from Virginia gentlemen to Tennessee pioneers, together with many of the wage workers in the towns.

When Washington saw this division coming on, he was deeply distressed. But his words were useless, because a free people must find a way to settle the natural conflicts that exist among them.

Thus the one-party Revolutionary government of the United States quickly split up into a two-party system.

In 1796 the Federalists won and elected John Adams as President. By 1800 the two parties were well separated and clear about their candidates for President and Vice-President. The Republicans won with Thomas Jefferson and Aaron Burr. Then all their electors voted for Jefferson and Burr. But since they could not state their preference the two winners were tied. The House, as provided in the Constitution, chose Jefferson. But Jefferson won over Burr only after thirty-five ballots in the House, showing that representatives of the losing party might easily be able to frustrate the intentions of the winning party by manipulating the votes in the House.

This absurd result led to the Twelfth Amendment, by which the electors now vote separately for President and Vice-President, and the winning candidates do not have to be sorted out by Congress. But this amendment wipes out the original purpose of the electoral college. It accepts the fact that parties exist and that the electors are only rubber stamps, bound to vote for the candidates chosen in advance by their parties.

At this point it may be well to explain why the party of Jefferson, which is now regarded as the ancestor of the present Democratic party, was originally called the Republican party.

In 1800, the Jeffersonians called themselves "Republicans," meaning simply that they were against kings. They also were in favor of the French Revolution, which they regarded as a good imitation of the American Revolution. The Federalists, on the other hand, were disgusted by the guillotine and the slaughter of the French aristocrats. They had a good deal of sympathy for the King of France. They accused the Jeffersonians of being "democrats," or lovers of the French Revolution. The word *democracy* at that time meant "mob rule" and was used much as we use the word *radicalism*. Later, after Napoleon had come and gone, the word lost much of its radical flavor. But when Jefferson was President, he did not call himself a "democrat," any more than Franklin Roosevelt would have called himself a "radical."

The Federalists were soon ruined by the success of the strong Federal Government which they had originated. Once the Federal Union was well established, the country grew rapidly. The people poured through the Appalachians into Ohio and Tennessee, and the back country began to outvote the Northeastern cities.

When Jefferson came into office in 1801, he did his part to promote the wave of American expansion. He laid aside some of his previous objections to a powerful Federal Government. He boldly bought "Louisiana," consisting of the whole Mississippi Valley west of the river.

The Federalists could not compete. Their party died off and did not even put up a candidate in 1820. Once more it was a one-party country. This period was called the "era of good feeling," because for a few years there was no opposition party. Instead, however, there was growing disagreement among the Republican leaders, and the two-party principle soon came back. The Republicans split into two factions. One, led by John Quincy Adams, and called National Republicans, took the more conservative side. Adams was elected in 1824. But in 1828 the other faction, calling itself Democratic-Republicans, won the Presidency with Andrew Jackson.

The National Republicans were succeeded by the Whigs in 1832. These so-called Whigs were not closely related to the Revolutionary Whigs, or "Patriots," nor to the Whigs of England. They were the conservatives, looking for a name that would attract votes. During this period the Federalist-National Republican-Whig party suffered because of the growing number of new frontier states that voted for the Jackson brand of politics. The Whigs, however, succeeded in electing two military heroes, William Henry Harrison in 1840 and Zachary Taylor in 1848.

In the 1850's the slavery issue grew more violent. Both the Whigs and the Democratic-Republicans, by this time called Democrats, were split by internal disagreements over slavery. The Northern and Southern Democrats were at odds. The Whig party broke up, and a new party whose central plank was antislavery, arose and named itself the Republican party. It nominated Abraham Lincoln and elected him to the Presidency in 1860.

As Washington had warned, the issue between the two parties in 1860, being "founded on geographical discriminations," and being so charged with emotion, was explosive. In addition to the emotional issue of slavery, there was the long-standing conflict between the high-tariff business interests of the Northeast and the low-tariff cotton interests of the South. Both these conflicts divided the nation into the same geographic regions. The opponents were therefore able to organize for a civil war, which they did as soon as Lincoln was elected.

The American people have not divided in the same way since the Civil War. Their sectional disputes have not been so bitter as to blot out the many other disputes which divide the people along other lines—such as the controversies over labor laws, spending, taxes, social security, or antitrust. In the main, the conflicts between rich and poor and between city people and farmers have outweighed those between North and South, or between the Northeast and the West. There has not been the setup for a civil war between sections.

The United States has also been secure against revolutions. Not since 1775 has there been the setup for an internal overturn, such as the Kerensky revolution in Russia or the Hitler or Mussolini revolutions in Germany and Italy. Whatever mob violence has occurred in the United States has been damped by the great size of the country and the fact that the violent disputes have not covered any large part of it. It is hard to imagine a march on Washington that could overthrow the government as Mussolini's march overthrew the government of Italy.

These fortunate circumstances go far to explain the way the present-day Republican and Democratic parties have come to be. After about a hundred years of experimentation with various forms of a two-party system, the American people happened upon a combination that would give play to a complicated network of political disputes, but with a good prospect of avoiding either civil war or revolution.

The modern two-party system as we have it in the United States has been built, more by instinct than by plan, as a way of achieving a majority government controlled by one winning party. Most of the time the President, the Senate, and the House of Representatives are all controlled by the same party. The minority party, meanwhile, is seldom so badly beaten as to suffer a widespread loss of hope.

This system contrasts with the usual multiparty governments of Europe on the one hand and the British two-party system on the other. The American system has a peculiar logic of its own which makes no sense to a European and not much sense to an Englishman.

In the typical European democracy there are many parties, and each one has a well-defined set of principles. One party may be Christian Socialist and another Catholic Conservative. By the curious twists of history, a party called Radical Socialists may well represent middle-class business interests. And always there are the Communists, who have the best discipline and will join with anyone who may be duped into pulling their chestnuts for them.

The theory of the multiparty system is that every party must stand for a principle, so that those who are for that principle can join and help promote it. Since modern life is complicated, and there are many political, economic, and religious principles, there can be many corresponding "splinter parties," and so there are.

But a democratic government of the parliamentary form has to have the support of a majority in its parliament. Any time that a vital bill proposed by the premier and cabinet fails to pass, the government must "fall." Either the premier and cabinet must resign, or, if their constitution permits, they may dissolve the parliament and call a new election.

In order to get a government, therefore, the usual democratic country in Europe has to put together a coalition of several parties, enough to make a majority. Each of these parties has its own pure milk of the Word; but it can never govern the country by that alone, unless it abolishes the parliamentary democracy and forms a dictatorship. In order to take part in a democratic government, it must dilute its pure milk with the muddy contributions of two or three other parties. There is, therefore, some tendency for different combinations to come and go without lasting long enough to hold a steady line of progress.

What is more discouraging, as it appears to Americans, is that where there are many parties, there is sometimes only one combination of the moderate, or "middle" parties, that can keep the country free.

As the picture is usually described, on the Right are the fascists, trying to overthrow free government and set up a new Mussolini or Hitler. On the Left are the communists trying to take over as they did in Czechoslovakia. This picture shows the parties favorable to democracy lined up in the middle, some leaning more to the right and some to the left.

This is a poor way to describe the arrangement of a set of parties, because it causes a dangerous tendency for the freedom parties to be pulled apart by the two totalitarian parties. The fascists or neo-Nazis, for instance, may lure some honest conservatives into their camp by saying that all "rightists" are on the same side at heart. The communists have all too often succeeded in making dupes of unwary liberals by calling all "leftists" into a united front. These maneuvers, if they succeed, would create what is called a "polarized" political situation, where the voters have to choose between fascist totalitarianism and communist totalitarianism. In order to avoid believing that there is only a choice between competing forms of suicide, it is best to avoid the figure of speech that seems to locate the free world hopelessly between the devil and the deep sea.

The better way to describe the arrangement of political attitudes is not as a straight line with fascists and communists on opposite ends, attacking the democratic forces in the middle. The true picture is more like a long thin triangle, with democratic institutions and parties on one end, and the competing totalitarians close together on the other. The fascists, or extreme reactionaries, and the communists, or extreme radicals, are both trying to set up a totalitarian police state. They are at odds merely like two underworld gangs, over the vital question of who is to control the racket. Often they join forces, as Hitler and Stalin did in 1939. In a parliament where the fascist and Communist parties have enough seats to be dangerous, they often are found voting together in the hope of bringing down the government.

Members of the antidemocratic parties easily jump from one to the other wherever they think they see the better racket. For instance, in East Germany the Communist government finds good use for many ex-Nazis, especially in its army.

To an American, the most dangerous weakness of a system of many parties is that the freedom of the country may come to depend absolutely at every election on the victory of the democratic "middle" group. That is, every election is a contest between freedom and disaster. The only choice is to jump out of the frying pan into the fire. Several European countries have been in that situation since World War II. Whether the people like the government or not, it is the only frying pan they have to sit in. If they fall out of that, they will land in the totalitarian fires that scorch the peoples of Eastern Europe.

The American system, imperfect though it is, has the virtue that it gives the people a choice between alternate ways of running a free government. The people may think that one party is better than the other at maintaining prosperity, or managing national defense, or avoiding waste and corruption. But the people believe—except at moments in the heat of an election—that even if the party they oppose finally wins, it will at least be pro-American and pro-democratic. There is no important suicide party that wants to deliver the country to the U.S.S.R. if it ever catches the people off guard and overthrows the party in power.

The price, however, of such a free choice is that both parties must be equipped with all the necessary leaders, followers, and principles for running the United States reasonably well. The winning party must subscribe, more or less sincerely, to all the well-established principles that the people require their government to uphold.

Once it is admitted that the American two-party system requires both parties to adopt practically all the principles and programs that any large block of voters may demand, the resemblance to Tweedledum and Tweedledee is seen to be sensible and necessary. Since each party, in advance of the election, is trying to show the voters a preview of itself as the government, it must show them a complete list of their more important requirements. It is therefore not surprising that American voters often feel that the Democratic and Republican platforms are practically alike, and that the parties merely have different candidates. The party is an organization for winning elections and getting control of the government, not for promoting one kind of ideology instead of its opposite.

It is not, however, absolutely true that the parties offer only their candidates, with identical principles and programs. Tweedledum is not absolutely the same as Tweedledee.

It is hard for an American to explain to a foreign visitor just what the real difference is between Republicans and Democrats—even to an Englishman who is used to a two-party system. Campaign oratory aside, there is some difference between the parties in the proportions of conservatives, liberals, and "sons of the wild jackass," as they have been called, and in their geographical location. The minority party usually wants to cut the budget more severely than the party in power, and it is usually more in favor of States' rights. There are many local or sectional interests that influence one party more than the other.

There are traces of the old distinction between the Federalists and Jeffersonians. Some of the Republicans seem to be more influenced by business interests and some of the Democrats more by labor; but there are numerous exceptions on both sides. As a matter of practice, it is usually found that important bills dealing with either foreign or internal questions split the majority and minority in Congress, and never in quite the same way.

In each party the voters who will always vote Republican or Democratic regardless of the candidates or issues do not make up a sure majority of the electorate. This also is a necessary feature of the two-party system as Americans understand it. If one party were to become the sure winner the voters would find themselves saddled with a one-party system. The one party would have to split in two, as the Democratic-Republicans did in 1824. When the two-party system is operating in healthy fashion, the election is decided by a middle group called the "independents"—people who look over the offerings of the two parties and then decide how to vote. In each election these independent voters usually accept some prevailing idea of the difference between the Democrats and the Republicans. Usually they regard the Republicans as more conservative than the Democrats, whatever that may mean to them at the time. Then they may be influenced by ideas about prosperity, or corruption, or peace; but most of all they choose between the presidential candidates.

In the United States the fact that some states are "solidly" Democratic and others "solidly" Republican is commonly regarded as a fault in the democratic system. These states have no real choice in the Federal elections, although locally they can choose between rival candidates in the primary elections of the dominant party. The democracy of the nation as a whole is saved by the fact that the one-party states do not dominate the national elections. The United States is fortunate in having no "solid" religious or racial group of any consequence that will vote as a bloc regardless of candidates or issues. Democracy, as the American people understand it, depends on having most of the elections decided by voters who make a free choice between candidates and policies.

In Britain there is a two-party system of a somewhat different kind. The British believe that the Labour and Conservative parties are far more different in policies and principles than the Democrats and Republicans. If so, this difference calls for some explanation.

Perhaps the best explanation is that in a proper two-party system, while the voters must be able to choose either party without starting a civil war, they want to see as much choice of different policies and attitudes as they can safely get. The United States has no serious dispute about its main direction of progress. Neither of the big parties wants to take the road to dictatorship, or to an economic collapse or any other general disaster. But this is a wide road, with fast and slow lanes and sometimes a chance for a detour or a short cut. The parties often represent a real difference in their attitude toward the fast and slow lanes, and that difference becomes a part of the people's choice in an election.

The opposition party picks its "issues," by measuring the criticisms and discontents among the voters that seem likely to draw support away from the party in power. But both parties try to avoid issues that would frighten away large numbers of voters. The effect of the choice of issues by practical politicians is that the parties are likely to differ as much as they can without being accused of "wanting to overthrow the Constitution."

If the British parties are further apart than the American ones, the reason would be that British political leaders can promise more drastic changes if they are elected, without scaring the public in ways that would lose the election. The British people, at least since the threatened rebellion in Northern Ireland on the eve of World War I, seem to be less excitable than the Americans. They can jump from Churchill to Attlee and back to Churchill without firing a gun. The Americans might not be able to take a socialist victory so calmly, but they can jump from Hoover to Roosevelt and from Truman to Eisenhower without a civil war. That is as good a definition as any of the correct distance between the two parties in a practical two-party system.

The Democratic and Republican parties, therefore, contain many discordant elements, in somewhat different proportions. They are always threatened with disruption. The force that holds the party together is, of course, that the leaders want to win the next election. But sometimes a rebellious leader walks out of the party and starts a third party, usually because he thinks the old party is too conservative. Thus Theodore Roosevelt split off from the Republicans in 1912 and founded the Progressive or Bull Moose party. Robert La Follette the elder campaigned as a Progressive in 1924; this also was a splinter from the Republican party. In 1948 the Democratic party gave off two splinter parties. The Wallace Progressives criticized the Democratic party as too conservative, and the Dixiecrats criticized it as too radical. None of these offshoots succeeded in destroying the old party and taking its place, though the defection of the Bull Moosers in 1912 defeated the Republicans and gave the election to Woodrow Wilson.

The fundamental weakness of third parties is that they always start with a conflict over a matter of principle and can attract only the voters who are devoted to that principle. Many of the followers of these splinter parties are frankly in favor of abolishing the Tweedle Brothers and rearranging the party system on grounds of principle.

They want to see all the conservatives in a conservative party, including the native fascists of the so-called right lunatic fringe; and all the liberals collected in a progressive party, which can welcome communists and the lunatic fringe of the left. Then, they say, the voters would have a real choice.

But this proposed separation of the sheep from the goats would be none other than the dreaded polarization, the wild logic of suicide. Somehow, any democracy that is fit to survive has to find some kind of party system that gives the people a chance to keep their freedom, however imperfect it may be. The American Republicans and Democrats have a system for persuading many conflicting interests to get along without shooting. It is full of faults and illogical compromises, but it has so far escaped disaster.

The majority of the practical politicians in the United States, who operate the two major parties, do not take kindly to the proposal for opposite and logical parties. When disgruntled voters break away and set up a third party, they do not slam the door. They prefer to offer compromises that will lure back into the fold as many third-party voters as possible. They close the door only on the third-party leaders when they think that they are wild men who would frighten other voters away. This preference for drawing discordant elements together is the main strength of the two-party system.

In addition to third parties, which try to challenge one of the major organizations, there are an indefinite number of minor parties. Some of these may be majors locally, such as the Farmer-Labor and Progressive parties that in the early years of this century were able to win State elections in the Midwest.

The Parties

Other minor parties are national in scope and seldom get more than a few hundred thousand votes. Their members do not expect to win even a State election—though the Socialists have controlled the cities of Milwaukee and Bridgeport for considerable periods. The small parties hope that by being on the ballot and organizing their small but enthusiastic following, they can persuade the major parties to adopt their program in the hope of getting their votes. The minor parties serve the purpose of allowing small groups to dramatize ideas not yet ready for adoption, without having to admit any of their leaders to the government itself. Most of the socialist proposals of the early 1900's, for example, are now planks in both the Democratic and Republican party platforms, though under other names. At one time the Prohibitionists saw their proposal adopted as an amendment to the Constitution. The Communist party, although it draws few votes, has probably had some influence on elections, either by throwing votes to a reactionary candidate or by poisoning a liberal candidate with unwelcome support.

Finally, the party system of the United States cannot be properly described without including the pressure groups that take an active part in elections. These organizations do not appear on the ballot. When they run a candidate for office, they do it indirectly by getting one of the major parties to nominate their man.

For example, the reason that there is no national labor party in the United States is that the American Federation of Labor long ago decided to let the two big parties bid for the labor vote. Labor leaders endorse the candidates that they regard as friendly, a Republican in one place and a Democrat in another. They believe that more is to be gained by having an influence on the winning party than by keeping the labor vote segregated in a losing party. Moreover, it is not clear that there is a "labor vote" in the United States. American workers do not always vote as their union leaders advise, an indication that "class consciousness," as it is called, is not as important in the United States as in some European countries.

Other organizations that take part in politics include the U.S. Chamber of Commerce and National Association of Manufacturers representing business; the Farm Bureau

Federation, the Grange, and the Farmers Union for agriculture; the League of Women Voters and General Federation of Women's Clubs, American Legion and Veterans of Foreign Wars, and the Daughters of the American Revolution.

The law attempts to make a distinction for tax purposes between organizations that work directly on the legislators to promote their own selfish interests and those that study public affairs for the good of the country. Contributions to political parties or to organizations classified as lobbies cannot be deducted from the income subject to Federal taxes.

The major political parties, therefore, operate in a complicated network of influences and pressures. They cater not only to the individual voter, as they understand his probable wants, nor merely to the sinister "interests" that pull hidden strings attached to the men in the "smoke-filled room." The two big parties are surrounded by minor parties and private organizations with all sorts of axes to grind, and each one claiming to have many thousands of voters tied up ready for delivery to the party that promises the right thing. The job of the party leaders is to make the correct combination of promises, and in the long run the correct performances, that will bring victory at the polls.

III.
PARTY ORGANIZATION AND OPERATION

WHEN THE PARTIES FIRST APPEARED IN AMERICAN PRESIdential elections, they had no nationwide organizations. There was only a division of opinion about national policies, with rival national leaders who wanted to be President. Congress divided itself into opposing groups which met in "caucus" and chose the candidates. But the caucus soon became unpopular. The party leaders who were not in Congress wanted a say not only in the election but in the nominations. Much of the history of party development has been made up of the struggles of expert politicians to control the nomination of candidates without unduly offending the voters and losing votes.

In 1824, the Democratic-Republican caucus disappointed the voters by failing to nominate Andrew Jackson. The mistake was remedied four years later, and Jackson was elected; but the caucus system of nominations had been discredited. The opposing parties then began to organize in conventions. Local conventions met and chose delegates to State conventions, and these in turn sent delegates to the national convention. The conventions chose party candidates for local, State, and national offices. This system was democratic in its own peculiar way, since it gave the working members of the party a chance to meet and vote, in their various levels of activity. On the other hand, the ordinary voter who was not a working member of the party never had any say except on Election Day. This also caused criticism and in course of time led to the adoption of a primary system in many States.

In most of the States we now have primary elections in the spring or early summer of election years, in which the parties choose candidates for local and State offices and for Congress. In some States the delegates to the national convention are elected in primary elections. They may be pledged to support a particular presidential candidate in the convention, at least for the first few ballots. The primary may also have a place on the ballot for the voters themselves to express their presidential preference.

The primary system has not, however, developed to such a point that any Republican or Democratic convention has met with its presidential nomination already in the bag. Candidates who have done well in the primaries but failed of nomination by the convention naturally want to increase the number and binding power of State presidential primaries. The professional politicians who are used to running the conventions prefer to keep the control in their own hands.

The national convention, so long as it retains the actual power to nominate the party's candidate for President, is a political ceremony of vast interest to the American public.

People watching the confused and noisy rabble on the floor of the convention often wonder how a great democratic nation can bear to have its President chosen in such a wild and howling mob. That, however, is to mistake the appearance for the real thing. The delegates on the floor are not choosing a President. They are getting acquainted with fellow members of the party and gradually working up enthusiasm, while the expert political leaders match their strength behind the scenes and try to find the candidate who will unite the party and win the independent vote. The leaders do not disregard the desires of the delegates, but they add them up in small meetings that do not show on the television screen.

Meanwhile on the floor, in the so-called demonstrations, the delegates are stimulated with bands, marching, and usually tropical heat as well. When the candidate is finally nominated, the war dance rises to a crescendo and lasts until large numbers of the defeated partisans are overcome with noise and excitement and join in the cheering and marching.

To many people viewing this orgy on the television screen it seems uncivilized, as indeed it is. But the war dance has a long and successful history in the development of the human race. Savage peoples all over the world have instinctively adopted the war dance as a means for unifying the tribe and rousing the laggards to go out and fight. The instinct of the political experts who created the national conventions is perhaps not to be cast aside lightly.

On the other hand, the use of television will undoubtedly change many features of the convention. It may change the common habit of sending a double contingent of delegates, each with half a vote. This feature lends itself to abnormally slow voting, and may sometimes be useful for political managers who are playing for time. It caters to the publicity hunger of delegates who, as one disgusted delegation leader said in 1952, "want on television." But it bores the television audience, and boring the voters is poor politics. The personal behavior of delegates on the floor of the convention is also likely to be improved by the knowledge that television cameras often have telescopic lenses, and that many deaf citizens are skilled in lip reading.

But whatever changes may be made in the technique of holding national conventions, it is doubtful if the party leaders will ever consent to letting the drama of the presidential nomination be taken away from the party acting in convention assembled.

At the convention the party also adopts its platform, or statement of principles. A committee on resolutions sits during the first few days of the convention. It listens to the representatives of labor, business, women's groups, Negroes, farmers, veterans, and anyone else who feels able to convince the committee that he can swing a block of votes in a closely contested State.

If the committee thinks it will get votes by giving the petitioner a "plank," or paragraph in the platform, it will do so, unless it "violates the principles of the party." What does that mean? Anything that will offend the rank and file of the party and cause large numbers to stay home on Election Day is a violation of the principles of the party.

For example, the planks in favor of "human rights," or legislation requiring equal treatment of minorities, were violently contested in the Democratic Convention of 1948. On one side were those who argued that millions of voters from the minority groups would be attracted by a strong human rights plank; and on the other those who threatened the loss of millions of "regular" members of the party. Similar arguments may occur in connection with labor or farm policies, especially if the people interested in the plank are in a position to play one party against the other, and so can demand a forthright statement.

Whenever possible, of course, the platform committee confines its output to phrases that will please without offending, with a special emphasis on the home, a balanced budget, lower taxes, and the American way of life.

The party, in fact, runs mainly on the "record," by which the orators mean a general claim that their own party is good, solid, and dependable. They hold their party up to be admired against a lurid background of the opposite party's actions that turned out to be unpopular with the voters. Each party has a traditional personality that it tries to maintain, in contrast with the miserable character of its opponent. The Republicans, for instance, picture their party as marked by efficiency and honesty, in contrast with the incompetent and half-communist Democrats. The Democrats tell the voters that they are the friends of the people; they stand for progress, as against the Republicans, friends of the rich, who "have to be dragged kicking and screaming into the twentieth century." Both parties include many distinguished members whose attitudes contradict these standard claims; yet the voters regard the conventional party characteristics as having some truth.

Few voters ever read the platform. It is sometimes quoted by political orators. If it includes anything that can offend a large group of voters, the opposing party will quote it. In practice, the candidate makes the working platform by his campaign speeches. He seldom directly contradicts the party platform, but he interprets it by omitting the parts he does not care to emphasize, and making statements of his own on the points he regards as important. After the election, the people regard the President's speeches as being the party's promises and look to him to persuade or bully the Congress into making the promises good.

The party convention, therefore, has only a secondary legislative power in adopting a platform that takes second place to the President's own program. Its real jobs are two: to select the candidate, and to unify the party in symbolic ceremonies.

The Vice-President, as a rule, is chosen by the presidential nominee and accepted by the exhausted delegates without much argument. The vice-presidential candidate is usually chosen with a view to pacifying the losing side in the convention. The effect is to put the winning faction of the party in danger of being reversed by the death of the President. Critics of this custom are constantly demanding some device for nominating a man who could have won in his own right if he had been nominated for the Presidency.

But the pressure to utilize the Vice-Presidency for unifying the party is a powerful obstacle to the free choice of a Vice-President.

Each party has a national committee that acts as the continuing organization between the conventions, since these come only every four years. Most of the committee work, however, is done in the year of the presidential election. The committee sets the time and place for the national convention. Its staff prepares campaign literature and sends out speakers. It raises some of the money for the presidential and Congressional campaigns.

The membership of the committee is made up of one man and one woman from each State, Territory, and island possession, chosen by the State delegation or by a State primary. Most of the work of the committee members is done in their home States where they co-operate with the State committees. The presidential candidate chooses the chairman of the national committee to run his campaign.

In addition to the chairman, who acts with the presidential candidate in planning the grand strategy of the campaign, the most important committee officers are the secretary, who organizes the immense correspondence of the central headquarters, and the treasurer, who raises most of the money.

A research staff collects the mass of information that candidates and other speakers need—the economic, racial, religious, and political characteristics of each district, the voting records of the Congressional candidates, and any other facts that will keep the speaker from giving offense and help him to attract votes. The committee also has expert writers to supply speeches for busy congressmen and senators, either for campaign purposes or between campaigns to support the party's side in Congressional debates.

In the Congress each party has a special committee with its own funds to help in the election of congressmen, and another committee to help the senators in their campaigns. These committees allocate money and speakers to the places where the elections are in doubt.

In each State there is a State committee for each party. These are, of course, most active in the States where there is a real contest. The organization reaches down to county committees and so on to cities, towns, and finally precincts, the areas that are served by each voting place.

The work at the precinct level is often called "doorbell ringing." The party workers try to persuade the people to register in time to be eligible to vote. They urge them to attend meetings when candidates come to town and, finally, to vote on Election Day. The organization at various levels above the precinct is largely devoted to serving the lowly precinct worker, by raising the money for the speakers, literature, radio, and television that back up the precinct workers' efforts to get out the vote.

The cost of running a national election is small, considering the size of the country and the number of people to be reached. Most of the estimates of total cost come to about 25 cents for everyone legally entitled to a vote, or something between 20 and 30 million dollars all told. In 1944, for instance, the Democrats officially recorded expenses of about $7,500,000, and the Republicans of $13,000,000. Each of the national committees is allowed to spend not over 3 million dollars in a campaign; but state and local committees collect their own funds. In addition, all sorts of people and organizations spend their own money and unpaid time in promoting their favorite candidate. The Hatch Act forbids Federal civil servants to work in a political campaign, but no way has been discovered to force every private citizen who takes part in a campaign to account for the time he spends or the money it costs him.

There is constant complaint about the vast sums of money that the other party is spending, and constant demand for laws to limit the costs of campaigning to what the less affluent party treasury can stand. But the actual buying of votes does not seem to be as common as in the past; and the feeling that the party with the big money will necessarily win the election is contradicted by numerous election results.

The chief trouble with getting the Government to help

Party Organization and Operation

with party financing seems to be that people feel shy about admitting that politics is a legitimate feature of government. In order for Congress to appropriate fifteen or twenty million dollars to each of the major parties, as has often been suggested, it would first of all have to throw off this feeling, coming down from George Washington himself, that parties are somehow indecent. Congress organizes its committees and chooses its operating officers on a party basis, but it feels embarrassed about mentioning parties in actual legislation. Another obstacle in the way of recognizing the parties as legitimate parts of the political system is the fact that many big contributors like it the way it is. They would rather put up the money for party activities than to see the parties independent of their aid.

As for a party trying to collect a dollar each from ten or fifteen million of the thirty million enthusiastic supporters who will vote for its candidate in November, experience has shown that it cannot be done at any reasonable expense.

The cost of national campaigns has become a more serious problem with the development of television. The people want to see the conventions on television, and they want to watch the principal candidates on the screen during the campaign.

It may be expected that as the demand for television views of the candidates grows, the honest use of campaign funds running as high as forty or fifty cents per adult American may not seem extravagant.

When the organization is well managed, smooth-running, and able to hold together from one election to the next, it is usually called the "machine."

The growth of political machines in the United States has been favored by the fact that elections for Congress come every two years, and often there are State elections in the odd years, as well as primaries. Only the great national convention, coming every four years, dies out between times. The national committees keep going in a quiet way between presidential elections, and the State and local machines are always on the job.

A machine is made up of a large number of professional political workers, who make their living by politics. It is therefore apt to defeat the reformers who are usually amateurs trying to overthrow the machine by spare-time political campaigns. The machine politicians do the hard routine work of scouting the community, keeping track of the maneuvers of their enemies, keeping in touch with all the interests, legal and illegal, that are affected by the enforcement of law, and coaching legislators and administrators on who is who and what is what. These workers are paid in various ways. Some have relatives on the public payroll. Some may even have jobs of their own at key points of political traffic in the Government. They may share in contributions from business concerns that need licenses or contracts or perhaps need only to be let alone by the police.

The best-running machines are led by a boss. The boss is usually not an officeholder. He is too busy with the strings that actually control the officeholders to spend time on the routine of a public office. The boss keeps his cohorts under strict discipline and in return gives them a leadership and co-ordination that will make them confident of success.

The boss is the man to "see," when any interest needs a political favor. He is also the friend of the people, especially of the poor, the foreign born, and the petty delinquent. More often than not the boss himself had a foreign-born father, and came up from the slums through the political machine by virtue of his organizing ability and his knowledge of the poor.

As the famous political expert George Plunkitt was quoted as saying: "If there's a family in my district in want I know it before the charitable societies do, and me and my men are first on the ground. I have a special corps to look up such cases. The consequence is that the poor look up to George W. Plunkitt as a father, come to him in trouble—and don't forget him on election day."

The job of the political boss is to comfort the distressed, whether they are poor or rich. With one hand he relieves the fears of a distracted immigrant mother whose son is in trouble, or sends coal or food to an old couple whom the respectable charities regard as "unworthy," or gets the party worker's son a job on the police force. For these services, generously given with no bitter sauce of moral judgment or charity, he gets the fervent devotion of his clients, and the votes of all their relatives delivered to whatever candidate he tells them is his favorite.

Party Organization and Operation

With the other hand he relieves the troubles of the rich and their allies— of contractors, traction companies, landlords, and saloon keepers, and possibly some less respectable citizens, who can get along if the law is not too strictly enforced. He passes the word to the men in the city hall or the State capitol who owe their election to the votes of the boss's friends and followers. He takes the grateful contributions of his moneyed clients and distributes the money to his workers and to the poor.

This old-fashioned, or Robin Hood, type of political machine has been undermined by social security, the immigration laws, and the merit system. There are fewer poor and bewildered immigrants in the big cities to whom the party workers can serve as the only friendly hearts in a strange land. There are also fewer "patronage" jobs that can be used for rewarding party workers. The police systems are still corrupt in many cities, and they are a strong support for the machine. But in the country as a whole the election of 1952 seemed to show that in the big cities where the Democratic machines had flourished during the depression, they had lost vigor.

Both of the major parties have made strenuous efforts to build amateur machines. They welcome the enthusiastic party supporters who will work for fun and for the chance to go to meetings and conventions, possibly someday to get a nomination. In 1952 both Eisenhower and Stevenson attracted great numbers of enthusiasts, including many young people. It is possible that in the future these amateur organizations are destined to play a larger part in the grass-roots work of getting out the vote. If this is so, it may represent a strange reversal in the wellsprings of political power. In the past, power has come up from the helpless poor, who could be bought with kindness and herded to the polls by the practical and corrupt machine politicians. This source of power has been drying up as the helpless poor have diminished in number. In 1952, the sources of power seemed to be concentrated in the presidential candidates. Both of them were chosen not to please the machines but to attract the independent voters and the middle-class, amateur party workers. These enthusiasts were moved not so much by gratitude or by hope of reward as by fervent admiration for their candidate. If this change is permanent, it may affect many of the working rules that have come down in the tradition of the art of politics.

The political parties have an important part to play in the actual conduct of the polling on Election Day.

In the United States there are about 130,000 precincts or election districts, in each of which some 300 to 1,000 voters cast their ballots. The polling place is usually in a school, a vacant store, or a firehouse or police station. Since women got the vote, the polling places have become strikingly cleaner than they were before 1920.

The election officials are selected by both the major parties and are paid from public funds as provided by State laws. They check the names of the voters, see that each voter gets one ballot, watch the ballot box or voting machine to prevent cheating, and finally sit up late in the evening to count and report the vote. The two parties usually post "watchers" at each polling place to challenge any signs of unfairness. The party pays the watchers.

The principle of the secret ballot is well established in the United States. Here and there the political machine may have methods for checking on how the voter is voting, but as a rule such methods are discouraged by the watchers of the opposite party.

A serious limitation on the American voting system is the "long ballot." It is not unusual for fifty to a hundred State, county, and city offices to be on the ballot that the bewildered voter is expected to mark. There is a record of one ballot twelve feet long with nearly five hundred names on it. The voters are asked to vote for half a dozen State officials in addition to the governor, and for county commissioners and judges, a treasurer and district attorney and several other officials. They have to choose a mayor, aldermen, members of the school board, city court judges, assessors, tax collectors, and dozens of others.

Only a professional politician is likely to know more than a few of the candidates for these offices, and he knows them because he had a hand in giving them the nomination. The voters vote for President, governor, mayor, and a few others, and either omit the rest or vote blindly.

The long ballot is preferred by old-fashioned politicians because it gives them freedom from responsibility to the people. They reward the faithful with nominations to the

Party Organization and Operation

minor offices that the public cannot remember or understand. Then the people blindly elect these officials. Being elected by the people, these friends of the political leaders are independent of the mayor or governor whom the people knowingly elected.

This system makes the State and local elections less democratic than the Federal. Nationally the people have only to vote for President—with Vice-President thrown in—and for congressman, and, two elections out of three, for senator. All these men are important enough to be visible and the people can hold them responsible for their actions.

The short ballot movement started early in the twentieth century to correct the evils of the long ballot. Woodrow Wilson was the first president of the Short Ballot Organization. Its purpose was to change most of the elective offices to appointive ones, so that the governor or mayor, like the President of the United States, would appoint the lesser officials and be the responsible head of an administration. But the politicians like the long ballot better. In the State governments, where the popular interest is weak and irregular, little progress has been made. In the cities the progress has been good. The mayor controls more of the appointments than in 1910, and in many cities the commission or city-manager forms of government give the voters the benefits of a short ballot.

It is probable that the long ballot has helped to reduce the size of the vote, especially among independent voters. A ticket with dozens of unknown names on it offends the voter who wants to pick and choose. It seems more natural to the voter who is in no doubt as to his party affiliation.

About three-quarters of all the voters are believed to be hereditary party members who would view with horror the idea of soiling their hands by voting for anyone in the opposite party. Elections, therefore, are decided either by the other 25 per cent, in the "two-party" States, or by factions in the one-party States who can fight over the nominations without going outside the respectable circle of their party. This all-important group of independents, which gives to national elections the uncertainty on which the democratic system depends, seems to be increasing.

In times of national crisis the political parties focus their drawing power in the person of their leader, the President or the presidential candidate. He is the one who must pull the hereditary voters from their armchairs on Election Day and get them to vote. He is the one who must win the votes of the independents, in competition with his rival, the leader of the other party.

After the election and the inauguration, the victorious President is expected to lead his party in Congress so as to get the legislation that he wants. The President in a time of crisis wants his place in history. As between an unwise campaign promise and what he afterward believes will make the best history, he will often choose the future rather than the past. In this endeavor he must deal with the leaders in Congress, leaders of his own party, often jealous of him, and opposition leaders who may or may not be inspired and led by their recently defeated presidential candidate.

This is the place of leadership in the parties in time of crisis, which, to younger Americans at least, seems to be the only kind of time there is. Older Americans can remember a different kind of time, such as 1920, when the people were tired after World War I and had no desire to be led anywhere.

The fact has often been noted that when the American people do not feel themselves in danger, the parties offer the voters figureheads with as nearly no leadership qualities as can be found. But when stormy weather comes up, they supply, by some mysterious process, men such as Lincoln and Wilson.

Many students have suggested that the process is less mysterious than it looks. The White House is the center of a world-wide net of information. There the facts of foreign and domestic situations, open and secret, are available to the President, digested into any form that he may require. More than one President who at first seemed a rather ordinary man has become a statesman almost overnight when the fearful stream of world knowledge was turned on him. It has been suggested that when there is no serious crisis, a President can be lazy and show no signs of greatness. But in time of storm, the same man might wake up and use the resources at hand for great deeds that his best friends would never have thought to be in him.

The organization and operation of the major parties may

Party Organization and Operation

be in process of transformation under the stimulating forces of present-day events. The continuous state of crisis, which has lasted since 1930 and seems likely to continue for many years to come, has placed a premium on both popular leadership and statesmanship in the White House and in Congress. Radio and television have reduced the opportunities and rewards of secret and shady deals in "smoke-filled rooms." The rise in living standards has reduced the "masses" who once were grateful to local political bosses, and who later followed President Roosevelt because he was their friend in time of need. Instead, these same people today are apt to live in pleasant houses and demand quite different political bait to lure them to the polls. The power of money in elections is still great, and the influence of contributors on both the parties is evident. But the voters appear to be sensitive to corruption, possibly more so than in times past.

The parties are thinking of new ways to organize their followers at the grass roots. The political scientists are urging the party leaders to find better ways of organizing the parties, so that they can work over their platforms, for example, by democratic methods of discussion. They say that a democratic system of conventions would pull the party members together and would bring more of their representatives to vote with the party in Congress and the State legislatures. There are signs that some of the party leaders are beginning to consider new ways. In many important respects the old traditional methods may be changing.

IV.
THE ADMINISTRATION

THE CONSTITUTION SAYS, "THE EXECUTIVE POWER SHALL be vested in a President of the United States of America." Congress and the President are almost always in some kind of conflict over what this "executive power" is. Because of the indefiniteness of the President's authority and the fact that it is held by a single person, he is apt to take over in any unusual situation for which no regular rules have been established.

The Constitution, to be sure, grants the President some definite powers. His veto of a bill is worth one-sixth of the voting strength of the Congress, since a bill passes with a bare majority if he says Yes and takes two-thirds if he says No.

The President has the initiative in foreign affairs. The Senate can block a treaty that the President has negotiated, but it cannot make a treaty or force the President to make one.

In the same way, the President is supposed to appoint the higher officers of the executive branch and the armed services, subject to Senate approval. But it often happens that a senator urges a candidate upon the President's attention, and the President cannot refuse without taking careful thought about how much the White House needs the support of the senator. There is also a custom called "senatorial courtesy." According to this custom, a senator of the majority party can block any appointment to a Federal job in his state by declaring that this man is "personally obnoxious" to him. His fellow senators will then do him the "courtesy" of refusing to approve the nomination. This custom, however, does not prevent the Republicans, when they are in power, making their own Federal appointments in the South, or the Democrats in their time doing the same in the Republican states of the North.

The Administration

John Locke, the English philosopher whose ideas strongly influenced the founders of the United States, described in his *Treatises of Government* the peculiar and illogical nature of the "prerogative," or executive power in England. Locke said:

"Prerogative was always largest in the hands of our wisest and best princes, because . . . it was visibly the main of their conduct tended to nothing but the care of the public. The people, therefore, finding reason to be satisfied with these princes, whenever they acted without, or contrary to the letter of the law, acquiesced in what they did . . . judging rightly that they did nothing herein to the prejudice of their laws, since they acted comformable to the foundation and end of all laws—the public good."

Locke also said that the legislative power is supreme and is "sacred and unalterable in the hands where the community have once placed it." Much of the political history of the United States, like that of England, is made up of the working out of this contradictory relationship.

In the United States, especially since radio and television have given the people a fairly close contact with their President, the boundaries of the executive power have more and more been located according to the people's judgment of the President. But even in our early history, the President sometimes acted "without, or contrary to the letter of the law."

For example, in 1793, when France declared war on Britain, President Washington proclaimed the neutrality of the United States. He had made up his mind that the American treaty of alliance with France did not apply when France was the attacker. Madison accused Washington of acting without constitutional authority and of imitating the royal prerogatives of the King of England.

Again, in 1803, President Jefferson suddenly got a chance to buy the territory of Louisiana from Napoleon, who was quite likely to change his mind if the offer were not snapped up immediately. Jefferson bought it. He privately admitted that this was "an act beyond the constitution" but he hoped Congress would back him up by letting him have the money. Congress backed him up; and that is how the United States happens to occupy the western half of the Mississippi Valley to this day.

Abraham Lincoln set aside the Constitution in probably more different ways than any other President, and the American people do not hold it against his memory. Lincoln suspended the right of habeas corpus, for example, in defiance of the Constitution, on the ground that the act was necessary to prevent the loss of the whole Constitution. He asked "Are all the laws *but one* to go unexecuted, and the Government itself go to pieces lest that one be violated? Even in such a case, would not the official oath be broken if the Government should be overthrown when it was believed that disregarding the single law would tend to preserve it?"

In 1917, before the United States entered World War I, Woodrow Wilson tried to get Congress to authorize him to arm American merchant ships. When Congress refused, Wilson turned to his authority as Commander in Chief and moved some of his armed forces aboard the merchant ships.

According to the Constitution the Congress has the power to "declare" war, and presumably the intention was to let Congress decide whether to go to war or not. But in fact any powerful element in the country may be in a position to get the United States into a war. Even the San Francisco Board of Education, responding to a widespread feeling in the State of California in 1906, ordered that Japanese children should be segregated from white children in the schools. This action set off a dangerous outburst of feeling in Japan. President Theodore Roosevelt sent a member of his cabinet to San Francisco, not that he had any power to force the Board to withdraw its order, but to satisfy the Japanese that he had tried to undo the insult.

The President can bring on a war by taking actions that are within his power and that create a war situation. Woodrow Wilson, for instance, protested against British and German violations of neutral rights, in terms that showed the gradual shift of American opinion from neutrality to an anti-German position. When he asked Congress for a declaration of war, it was too late to refuse. On the other hand, in 1812 the majority of Congress hotly desired war with England. Some historians have thought that President Madison was unwillingly dragged into the War of 1812.

The Administration

Often, in fact, the President is obliged to decide questions of war or peace without waiting for Congress and the American public to debate the question. On several occasions before Pearl Harbor President Franklin Roosevelt took quick action against Hitler that could have been blocked by delay. Such actions included the seizure of a German outpost on the Greenland coast and sending troops to defend Iceland. President Truman had similar emergencies to handle at the start of the Berlin blockade and again when the Communists attacked South Korea. These were both probing raids against the free world, like the Japanese, Italian, and Nazi aggressions that led up to World War II. If the Soviets had not been instantly answered in Berlin and Korea, the world would have been on the slide leading to World War III. No one but the President of the United States, acting in his own right, was in a position to meet those emergencies.

Even when the President has a Constitutional power to act, a hostile Congress may block him by refusing him the money to carry out his policies. When President Truman sent American troops to Europe to bolster the infant defense force of NATO, he was acting as Commander in Chief, as many Presidents have done in the past when they have thought best to land troops on foreign soil. There was a great debate in Congress about whether the President was within his rights, and some of his political opponents tried to tie his hands by cutting off the money. The struggle was more political than legal.

The President's relations with Congress are a mixture of the struggle for power between the executive and legislative and the complicated struggle for political advantage. In a parliament most of the prime minister's party followers will stand by him, since if he loses a crucial vote, he and his party will be out of power. But in Congress, as a rule, a proposal from the White House will split both parties. Some members agree or disagree with the President; others vote for or against his policies because of party reasons. The real forces at work are not to be found by reading the Constitution. If the President is skillful at the art of making friends in Congress, even in the opposition party, he can get many votes by friendship alone. If the President has many Federal appointments to hand out, and has not yet announced his choices, he can buy some votes by giving his enemies the privilege of putting their constituents on the payroll. It is noticeable that a congressman whose principles force him to side with the President does not get as many jobs to hand out as a hostile member of the President's party. The squeaky axle gets the grease.

Every President, therefore, is said to have a "honeymoon" when he first comes into the White House. This is the period when he still has plenty of new jobs with which to pacify his enemies. Once his stock of appointments runs low, the traditional conflict between Congress and the White House is renewed. From there on the President has to depend on his charm and on the backing of the people.

President Franklin Roosevelt started the serious use of radio with his "fireside talks." In many a hard-fought struggle with an angry and snarling Congress, Roosevelt was able to get the measures he wanted because his enemies in Congress were afraid of the people at home.

On the other hand, the people will rise to defend any congressman or senator in the President's own party if the President tries to "purge" him. In 1938 Roosevelt tried to get the voters to defeat certain Democrats who opposed his policies, and practically all were re-elected with stinging majorities. The President must not break the united front of his party when it goes to the polls, although he can sometimes use his influence against an enemy inside the party, especially in secret.

The universal opposition to presidential purges evidently rests on a deep instinctive respect for the peculiar logic of the American two-party system.

The Cabinet is not the same kind of institution as the Cabinet in a parliamentary democracy such as Great Britain. In particular, the heads of departments are not members of Congress, and do not appear on the floor of the House to be questioned. The President chooses his Cabinet as the result of a complicated calculation in which fitness for the job is only one consideration. The Cabinet jobs must be well distributed among the States or regions where the vote is worth fishing for, and also among the important religious and economic groups. Cabinet members seldom come from the solidly Democratic South or from solidly Republican States such as Maine or Vermont,

The Administration

since it is a waste of political resources to cater to the local patriotism of States that always vote the same way.

The regular departments, headed by Cabinet members, are almost entirely under the President's direction, and he can remove any Cabinet member for refusing to carry out a duty that is based on the President's constitutional powers. Originally, only the State and War departments were created to be definitely subordinate to the President. They represented branches of his own Constitutional powers. The Secretary of the Treasury was directed to report to Congress, since his duties were based on Congressional powers. But President Washington started a process of pulling the Cabinet into Presidential control, and no one now questions the President's authority over the departments in general. On the other hand, Congress can create new duties based on the powers of Congress and entrust them directly to a Cabinet officer or a bureau head. The extent of the President's power to direct or discipline an officer in the exercise of such responsibilities has not been entirely settled.

Congress has created a large number of emergency and independent agencies, such as the Works Progress Administration of 1935, to give work to the unemployed, and the Federal Trade Commission, to regulate certain practices of private industry. The relations of these agencies to the President have raised many problems that the courts have not been able to answer clearly.

Some agencies, such as the Rural Electrification Administration, are public services that can be placed in an ordinary department and controlled by the President as head of the national administration. Others are not so clearly suitable for direct Presidential control. The Civil Aviation Board and the Federal Communications Commission are given power to make rules for the operation of airplanes and radio stations, respectively, which have the force of law. These agencies must hold hearings and decide what the facts are, making their decisions according to broad principles laid down by Congress. As a rule the President has less authority to direct or discipline such agencies than in the case of ordinary Federal services.

Then there are half-judicial agencies, such as the Federal Trade Commission, that can hold hearings and declare that a private concern is violating the law and must change its way of operating. The Supreme Court has decided that the President has no power to dismiss a commissioner of the FTC for actions that the President disapproves.

The theory of this peculiar mixture of legislative, executive, and judicial bodies has baffled the courts. The practical aspect is less difficult to understand. The officials, whether controlled by the President or not, are chosen by the President and confirmed by the Senate. The political reality is illustrated by the case of the Federal Power Commission, which regulates, among other things, the interstate traffic in natural gas. The commission having refused to give the gas companies the rates they wanted, the companies appealed to Congress and got it to pass a bill removing the question at issue from the commission's control. President Truman vetoed the bill, and Congress failed to pass it over the veto. Then one of the commissioners who had voted against the gas companies came to the end of his term and was reappointed. The gas companies persuaded the Senate to refuse to confirm this commissioner. Finally a different commissioner, favorable to the companies, was appointed and confirmed. This appointment reversed the majority. The commission then took the gas-company point of view, and all was once more quiet on that front. The moral of this story is that any commission or even any court will follow the election returns, if not immediately, at least by the process of replacement of its members.

In the levels of administration below the policy-forming, or political officers, are the nonpolitical civil servants, the routine workers from messengers and janitors up to research experts and supervisors. If the civil servants have any political preferences, the law allows them to vote in their home states but not to take an active part in politics.

Politics, however, sometimes interferes with the efficiency of the civil service.

If left to itself, without Congressional attention, the civil service has two principal forces working for and against efficiency. In favor of efficiency is the considerable body of expert supervisors and personnel officers who know how to manage government employees, together with the top executives who understand and support the expert managers. The system for encouraging good management and exchanging technical knowledge on efficiency methods was pulled together and streamlined in 1947 by an executive order of President Truman. This order provided for delegating authority to the agencies; for setting standards of management that would help improve performance, and for inspection by experts, similar to the most modern practice in private insurance companies and banks. There are many spots in the Federal Administration where high efficiency is found, and the methods used are not infrequently copied by private business concerns.

The internal force that operates against government efficiency, just as in private business, is made up of executives who do not understand modern methods of handling their people. Officials who are appointed for political reasons, or even for superior abilities in military planning or foreign affairs, may have no knowledge of the art of management. The President cannot pick his Cabinet solely on the basis of their knowledge of how to run a large organization at a low cost.

The effect of Congressional interest in the cost of running the government is generally to reduce the efficiency of the civil service. Modern methods of operation, as they are illustrated by the most efficient private enterprises, are based on a policy of politeness toward employees. A typical courtesy is to allow a "break" for coffee in the middle of the forenoon. The effect of courteous management is higher production at less cost. But such methods offer easy targets for political attack.

A politician can get votes by sternly accusing the bureaucrats of laziness and dishonesty. Where accurate records of output are kept, a loss of as much as $100,000 has been noted as a result of one speech in Congress attacking a certain agency.

On the other hand, a Congressional investigation fairly and honestly carried out can sometimes save money by uncovering waste in agencies where the head is not a good manager.

The best hope for improving the effects of politics on the civil service would seem to lie in getting the help of prominent businessmen who have learned the modern principles of efficiency. When enough of these men turn their attention in the direction of this problem to exert a strong influence on Congress, they may be able to discourage political raiding. They may also be expected to exchange technical knowledge on a wider scale with the good managers in government and lend them much-needed support.

The size of the Federal Administration is always a source of anxiety, not only because of its cost, but even more because of its "bureaucracy." Bureaucracy is a word used in the American language to indicate the fear that vast government agencies, employing thousands of people, may be lost in the confusion and may escape the knowledge of Congress or even the President. There is a suspicion, not always without cause, that some of these agencies, set up to deal with some long-ago emergency, have continued to live an almost independent existence because no one has found them and told them to close up shop.

Another common belief, somewhat better founded, is that different agencies, set up at various times, have often developed their work so that it overlaps. Sometimes an agency in its present form seems to be in the wrong department where its work is not properly related to other work of a similar kind.

All recent Presidents have tried to reorganize the executive branch so as to make it more logical and efficient. President Hoover brought the scattered veterans' agencies together into the Veterans' Administration. He obtained a Reorganization Act in 1932 allowing him to shift various bureaus about, subject to a check by Congress. All such plans were to be laid before Congress and would become valid if not disapproved in sixty days.

The House had gone Democratic in 1932, and it refused to accept Mr. Hoover's plans, wanting to leave reorganization to the new Democratic President.

President Roosevelt appointed a committee in 1936 to study reorganization. It reported in 1937 with far-reaching recommendations, which met with strenuous opposition from the President's opponents. A much watered-down bill was passed in 1939, and under it the President succeeded in making some changes. He transferred the Budget into the Executive Office of the President, for example. During the war he also consolidated housing and shipping agencies into the National Housing Agency and the War Shipping Administration and made other reforms under his emergency war powers.

President Truman obtained a Reorganization Act in 1947 under which he appointed a bipartisan commission with Former President Hoover at its head. The Hoover Commission made a thorough study and offered suggestions that Hoover estimated could save the Government $3,000,000,000 a year. The Hoover report was well received by the public. President Truman submitted about twenty plans to Congress, and Congress allowed three-fourths of them to stand. In 1953 Congress extended the reorganization law for President Eisenhower.

The benefits of rearranging the bureaus and agencies are never so striking as to attract enthusiastic support from the public, but some of the most glaring defects in the Administration have been corrected by these changes. Some agencies, however, such as the Corps of Engineers, have such powerful political backing in Congress that no President has been able to impose any changes against their opposition.

Economy, or not buying what the people don't want, is the job of Congress; but the President can baffle the Congressional desire to get credit for cutting expenses by presenting a "tight" budget, containing little or nothing that the people do not want. Efficiency, on the other hand, meaning to get the most for the least money, is the job of the President. To some extent, Congress can baffle the President by penny-pinching and by throwing in wasteful provisos to please some special interest. But on the average, President Hoover and his successors can be said to have made some progress toward both good organization and modern management.

V.
CONGRESS—WHAT IS IT?

THE UNITED STATES CONGRESS DIFFERS FROM A PARLIAment chiefly in the fact that it does not contain the executive. The President and his Cabinet are not members of the House, as the Prime Minister and his Cabinet are in England. The Congress cannot peremptorily ask a question of the President except in an impeachment proceeding; and if it refuses to pass an Administration bill, there is no "crisis." The President in that case does not resign; nor does he dissolve Congress and force a new election.

In the United States Government, the people are represented in one way by the Congress and in another by the President. Each has the right and the means to appeal directly to the people for support against the other, and they do. The effect is that the struggle between the executive and Congress varies between open hostilities and an armed truce, even when the President's party is in control of Congress. Another situation, that cannot occur in a parliament, arises when the people choose a President of one party and a Congress of another, putting the executive and the legislative branches automatically in opposition to each other.

The United States Congress is therefore more irresponsible than a parliament, for the members of the President's party can vote against an Administration proposal without voting to have the President resign. This lack of responsibility encourages demagogues in Congress to play for headlines, since the party in power does not feel that strict discipline is a matter of life and death.

Woodrow Wilson, when he was a college professor, advocated a constitutional change that would have given Congress the powers and responsibilities of a parliament. He argued that if the Congress had to pass the President's bills or else face a crisis, it would take its work more seriously and the people would watch it more intelligently.

Congress—What Is It?   57

When Wilson became President he thought of forcing a crisis in case of a balky Congress. He could have resigned with the Vice-President and all the Cabinet. Thus all the heirs to the Presidency, as the law then stood, would vanish, and Congress would have to choose a new executive. But he had a war on his hands and could not afford to upset the established order of business. There is no noticeable public demand in the United States for the transformation of the Congress into a parliament.

One effect of the separation of powers is that the Senate is as important a body as the House. In other countries there is a tendency for the lower house, since it controls the executive, to assume all the power, letting the upper house live on as a debating society of elder statesmen. In England, for instance, the House of Lords has been stripped of its veto power. It may delay a bill by voting against it; but the House of Commons has the final word. The United States Senate is as powerful as the House, and in some respects more so.

The tradition of a two-chambered legislature is deeply rooted in American political life. The colonial governments had two chambers and so do all the States except Nebraska. But the principal reason that no one can conceive of any movement toward a one-chamber Congress is that the United States is still a Federal Union of large and small States. No other method of solving the problem of uniting big and little States that would satisfy the American people has been suggested.

The fact that all bills have to pass two different bodies does not cause delay in emergencies when the people are united in favor of following the President's leadership. But on ordinary matters in ordinary times, legislation is slow, hearings are duplicated, and the opposition has an advantage over the proposition. In the light of the American prejudice against all governments, the fact that controversial laws do not pass easily is regarded without dismay. And it is a proverb that two heads are better than one.

The Senate and the House of Representatives differ in their composition and attitude, even though the Constitution has been amended to shift the election of senators from the State legislatures to the plain voters. The senators average a few years older than the congressmen. Congressmen often move up into the Senate, but few ex-senators have ever run for Congress. The senators are more distinguished by their office because there are only 96 of them while there are 435 congressmen. A seat in the Senate has a high publicity value which can be used for good or ill purposes.

The Senate's power of approving treaties and of confirming presidential appointments has caused many senators to pay special attention to foreign relations and to the make-up of the Administration. Some of them have become distinguished authorities on these subjects.

More than half of the members of the Senate and House are lawyers. A lawyer can serve a term in Congress and if he is then defeated for re-election can return to his law practice with usually an improved chance of earning a living. Moreover, it is not illegal for a member of Congress to keep his partnership in a law office, where contributions from persons interested in legislation can be received in the form of "retainer fees." Such connections are frowned upon in the case of civil servants or officials in the executive branch.

A schoolboy is said to have stated that "ours is a government of lawyers, not of men." In general this is an exaggeration; but there is no doubt that Congressional opinion on many great questions, such as economic policies and international co-operation, often bears the marks of the lawyer's mind rather than of the engineer's, the businessman's, or the journalist's habits of thought.

Congress and the President are the two great instruments through which the national political parties govern the country and struggle for power. The President, being a single person, represents a party position that is apt to be definite and closely connected with his personal re-election or his idea of a desired place in history. The President's party in Congress, on the other hand, always includes some individuals who oppose the President's policies in one way or another. It also includes many individuals who believe their re-election will depend on local interests that may be opposed to the position of the party in general. The party in power therefore is split on nearly all Congressional balloting; and so, for that matter, is the party in opposition.

The responsibility of Congress comes home to roost only every two years, and then in a general and somewhat in-

Congress—What Is It?

definite way. Many individual votes in Congress will not have any noticeable effect on the next election as a whole, though they may be the deciding factor in a congressman's home district. This fact makes for lack of discipline. Many congressmen, too, have come from "safe" districts, which will surely re-elect them if they do not offend the home folks; and that they are hardly likely to feel moved to do. They are almost entirely independent of their national party, except for the fact that if their party loses the election they will lose their committee chairmanships. The responsibility of Congress to the sovereign people, therefore, is found in only a shadowy form in the States and districts that elect their representatives for unchanging local reasons. The sovereign people actively pass judgment on their Congress only when there is a close contest, and then only when the record of a candidate is definitely related to the issues that the people think important.

In a doubtful State, the independent voters, who feel free to vote without regard to any party loyalty, can usually decide the election. Or if the State is dominated by one party, the independents can, if they choose, join the dominant party and have an important influence in its primaries.

But, as Lowell Mellett has pointed out in his *Handbook of Politics,* the independents often throw away their power by dividing their votes. Independents are often "liberals" who can easily believe that it is their duty to vote for the best man among the candidates in a primary. Often in an election they will cast enough "protest" votes for one of the small splinter parties to have decided the election had they supported one of the major party candidates.

The regular party politicians sometimes take advantage of this habit of the independents. The party that fears the independent vote may outwit the independents by quietly supporting an additional candidate who cannot win, but who will attract those who want to vote for the "best man."

As Mellett says, the effective way for independents to use the balance of power when they have it is to agree among themselves on whether they approve of the man now in office, assuming that he is running for re-election. Then if they like him they can join in keeping him there, where he will gain in seniority and influence. If they do not like him, they can unite in voting for the challenger who is most likely to win, whether he is the "best" man in the race or not. For no matter how undesirable a candidate may be, if he defeats the man in office he comes to Congress as a "freshman" with no seniority.

These relationships of the sovereign people to their legislative agents may seem dangerously loose. But they square with the fundamental democratic principle set forth in the Declaration of Independence, that the Government derives its just powers from the consent of the governed. In the States and Congressional districts where one party always wins, the governed have simply given a blanket consent to the position of their own party without further argument. They can withdraw that carte blanche any time they feel so inclined. Moreover, the principal feature of democratic government is that not only those who fail to vote, but those who vote and lose the election must peacefully consent to be governed by the winners. This result is fully obtained by the Congressional elections, whatever other weaknesses the system may show.

If, after making his own record, the President is approved by the people, and his party again captures the White House, his success is a help to the congressmen of his party. The closely fought Congressional contests are apt to swing toward the side that is winning the Presidency. This is called "riding in on the President's coattails." The coattail principle undoubtedly has some effect toward winning the loyalty of congressmen and senators to the leader of their party. If they hurt him too much, they may hurt themselves. It is a notable fact that the party that holds the White House nearly always loses seats in the "mid-term" elections, when the Presidency is not being contested.

The party leadership in Congress is usually chosen from those who will support the President, but some of the committee chairmen, who have vast powers in their various fields, may be wholly opposed to the White House. In 1953, for instance, at the very start of President Eisenhower's Administration, his policy of balancing the budget before cutting taxes was bitterly opposed by the Chairman of the House Ways and Means Committee.

Such evidences of indiscipline, with their risks of possibly dividing the party in the next election, have led to many

Congress—What Is It?

proposals for more effective party organization. At times the party caucuses or policy conferences in the two houses have tried to bind their members to follow the decision of the party. But there has to be an escape clause for those who have some pledge or other obstacle that forbids them to vote that way. The trouble with all attempts to impose discipline is the lack of penalties that can be imposed on those who stray. The chief difficulty is that the national party leaders cannot read a man out of his party in his home state. If he wants to call himself a Democrat and then vote with the Republicans, no one can stop him so long as the people at home re-elect him. All the party can do is to throw him off committees, as the Republicans did with Senator Morse in 1953.

All in all, the lack of discipline is a logical consequence of the American two-party system operating in a Congress that does not have parliamentary powers and responsibilities.

The party opposed to the President is usually, but not always, in the minority in both houses of Congress. The proposition that the duty of the minority is to oppose is only partly true. It is, to be sure, a duty of the opposition to see to it that doubtful questions are thoroughly discussed, and that doubtful practices in the Administration are thoroughly investigated. But the opposition is complicated by the divisions in the minority party, and by the conflicts between the President and the majority party. Some members of each party can be counted on to vote against their own party on most of the issues. And among the most loyal members of the minority party the question often arises: "Shall we oppose the President or oppose his party?"

From 1933 to 1952 the general policy of the Republicans was to oppose the President. When the President was having trouble with Congress, many of the Republicans voted with the Southern Democrats who were the President's usual opponents in his own party. This policy for a long time failed to win elections because the people were more attached to the President than to the Democratic party in Congress. It finally succeeded when criticism of the Administration took effect on the voters.

When the President is faced with a Congress controlled

by the opposite party, the normal hostility between Congress and the White House is heightened, but there are limits. No politicians, except the few members of the "lunatic fringe," want to carry their war against the President to a point that would endanger the security of the nation. In law, a hostile Congress has a right to cut off appropriations and a hostile Senate could refuse to confirm the President's Cabinet; but sane members of Congress do not regard extreme tactics as good politics for the long pull. As a result, the war is less than total.

In the Eightieth Congress, for example, Mr. Truman was able to get the Marshall Plan approved, thanks to the enlightened leadership of Senator Vandenberg on the Republican side. The senator persuaded his party not to fight on an issue where it had little to gain and much to lose. For one point, if the Plan had failed, and if Italy had gone Communist in the elections of 1948, those who were responsible for defeating the Marshall Plan would have been blamed in the United States for the disaster in Italy.

But on domestic issues, the Republicans in control of the Eightieth Congress and the Democratic President were in a cold war of no mean proportions. The President demanded all the measures that had any popular backing, including those that a Democratic Congress would have failed to pass. As the Republican Congress, with considerable help from Democrats, turned down each demand, Mr. Truman wrote down one more note in his campaign notebook. Thus the Republicans, although they were able to block most of Mr. Truman's policies, failed to make Mr. Truman take the blame, and he won the election.

On the other hand, in 1932, when President Hoover was faced by a hostile Congress, the Democrats were able to frustrate his final efforts to deal with the depression and to leave him carrying the blame. This situation has occurred often enough to create a legend that a President whose party loses control of Congress at the mid-term election is doomed to defeat two years later.

It may seem strange, with the constant strife between the two parties cutting through the struggle between President and Congress, that the Government manages to get anything done. The forms of conflict have been outlined here to bring out the importance of the political side; but there are many influences working toward a final agreement and practical action. One is the fact that there are conservatives and liberals in both parties. The President nearly always gets some support from the opposition. This may be illogical, but it creates an obstacle to all-out war between contending factions. More important, the majority of those who become leaders in Congress are practical politicians who have risen to power by their skill in the art of compromise.

VI.
CONGRESS AT WORK

EVERY TWO YEARS A NEW CONGRESS IS ELECTED. THE Eighty-second Congress, for instance, was elected in 1950, and the Eighty-third Congress in 1952. All the members of the House and one-third of the senators are chosen at each election.

Congress is required to meet at least once a year. It regularly meets on January 3. The first session of a new Congress "organizes" itself, electing its officers from the majority party and distributing the committee chairmanships and memberships.

The Vice-President of the United States is president of the Senate, and has the deciding vote in case of a tie. His other duties are indefinite. The White House may use the Vice-President as a contact man among the senators, or he may sit with the Cabinet and become a sort of understudy to the President. A Vice-President who has been a senator can sometimes exert a considerable influence among his former colleagues.

The Senate elects a president pro tempore, who serves in the absence of the Vice-President. Other elective officers are the secretary and the sergeant at arms, who manage the routine work of the Senate, the chaplain, and the secretaries of the majority and the minority. Most of the Senate organization, including the committee chairmanships, will hold over from one Congress to the next, unless there is a political overturn.

The caucus of the majority party nominates the officers, committee chairmen, and majority committee members. As a rule they are elected on the first ballot by the whole Senate. The minority party chooses the members who are to represent it on the committees. Seniority is an important factor. The chairman of a committee is almost always the majority member who has had the longest service on that particular committee. Seniority also gives a senator the right of preference in choosing his committee posts.

In the House the presiding officer is the Speaker, who is elected by the members and is always a member of the majority party in the House. The Speaker is now first in line of succession to the Presidency in case of the death of both President and Vice-President. His is also the most powerful office in the Congress.

Although the name of the office is inherited from England, the nature of the Speakership is not the same. The House of Commons chooses a Speaker for his impartiality and ability as a presiding officer. In the United States Congress the Speaker is one of the most important agents of party control. He appoints the members of conference committees, for example. These men meet with a corresponding group of senators to iron out the differences between House and Senate bills covering the same subject. Their combined version is usually passed by both houses, and the decision on some of the most vital issues may therefore depend on who is chosen by the Speaker to go to the conference.

The Speaker can arbitrarily decide who shall be recognized and allowed to speak from the floor. If there is doubt as to which of two committees is the proper one to consider a bill, the Speaker can decide where to send it; and that may mean committing it to a friendly or a hostile committee. The Speaker can take part in debate by appointing a substitute and descending to the floor.

Before 1910 the Speakership developed into an iron rule in the hands of Thomas B. Reed of Maine and "Uncle Joe" Cannon of Illinois. Speaker Cannon appointed all members of standing committees. He served as Chairman of the Rules Committee, which had the power to prevent action on any bill. In 1910 a coalition of Democrats and Western "insurgent" Republicans succeeded in putting the Speaker off the Rules Committee, and later they took away his power to appoint the standing committees.

In the House, as in the Senate, seniority is the most important element in filling the principal offices, particularly the committee chairmanships and the membership of most powerful committees. As a result, the most strategic offices in Congress are usually held by older men who have come from "safe" States that re-elect their representatives for life.

In addition to the officers and committees, both Senate and House have party organizations that are powerful in the control of legislation.

Each party is organized in each House in what the Republicans call a conference and the Democrats a caucus. The party not only nominates its members for official posts; it also chooses its floor leader and assistant floor leader, or "whip." The floor leader is the general in charge of party strategy on the floor, deciding which members are to speak and when, and whether to hasten or delay action. The whip keeps track of the members and brings them in when they are needed for a vote.

The majority party in the House has a steering committee, headed by the floor leader, which works closely with the Rules Committee to promote the bills that the party conference or caucus has decided to favor. In the Senate both parties have steering committees, but they are less powerful because senators are less easily controlled.

The party organizations have a strong but not always controlling influence on legislation, especially on "party" issues, where each party has a well-defined policy in conflict with the other party. On such issues the party organizations contribute by managing the debate and mustering their members. But often the question at issue splits both parties, and the party organization tries to make the will of the older and more powerful members prevail. It is not unusual for the controlling elements in the two parties to act informally in coalition against the younger men of both. Thus in Mr. Truman's time there were often signs of cooperation between the conservatives of both parties in opposition to the President.

Tourists who visit Washington and go to watch the Senate or the House from the galleries are usually shocked at the scene on the floor. Usually when a member is making a speech, most of the seats are empty. The members who are present are reading or wandering about talking with one another. A few are attending to the speaker and interrupting him frequently, sometimes to take his side but more often to contradict his argument. Then comes a roll call for a vote or for a quorum. The bells ring throughout the Capitol and the office buildings, and the members soon come crowding in to answer to their names. They soon drift out

Congress at Work

again, and the normal appearance of nonchalance is resumed.

The vast majority of senators and congressmen work long hours and under harassments from eager constituents that would soon wreck the nerves of a quiet man. The scene on the floor does not give a fair picture of how the Congress works. Most of the time there is no great debate that will influence the people of the whole nation and possibly even a few congressmen. Most of the time the floor is a place where the member goes to answer the roll call, to make a speech for the record or interfere with another member's speech, and incidentally to get a few words with fellow members whose help he may want on some coming legislation. The floor is the market place but the goods that come to market are manufactured elsewhere, mainly in the committees and the lobbies.

The Senate and the House both have standing committees on the principal subjects of legislation. When Congress was reorganized in 1946, the standing committees in the Senate were cut from 33 to 15, and in the House from 48 to 19. The idea was to reduce overlapping and also to give each member a chance to belong to fewer committees and concentrate his work. This reform was not as drastic as it looked, since the committees promptly created new subcommittees.

There are also a number of joint committees with members from both houses. They deal with comparatively dull subjects such as printing or the Economic Report, in which there is less political nourishment for aspiring politicians than in taxation or the armed forces. Joint committees avoid duplication of hearings; but on matters loaded with political controversy the reasons that justify having two chambers in the Congress can be said to justify two sets of hearings on the same subject.

In the reorganization of 1946, Congress promised itself not to indulge in the creation of special committees. These had been much used in past years, mainly for investigation. They had the advantage that the member who persuaded Congress to authorize the investigation was usually made chairman and could be counted on to do a job.

Senator Truman, for instance, was chairman of a committee to investigate the conduct of World War II, and succeeded in preventing or stopping many cases of inefficiency or graft. This work led him to the Vice-Presidency and the White House.

Although few special committees have been appointed since 1946, special or permanent subcommittees have sometimes been appointed for similar purposes.

The ordinary process of writing legislation requires long and hard study by the committees. Many of the important bills are suggested by the President, and the agency most concerned is likely to send up a proposed draft of a bill. But these drafts are only the beginning. The committee in charge of the bill must satisfy itself that it will take responsibility for every word of its own final draft before it goes to Congress.

The committees usually hold hearings, some of them open and others secret, depending on the subject matter. At these hearings the heads of executive agencies and their experts are questioned—not always with success in drawing out all the facts, for the congressmen are usually less familiar with the subject than the experts. The same may be said of the questioning of lobbyists, the paid advocates of private interests concerned with the bill. Most of the open activity of the lobbyists is made up of arguing before committees, but the lobbyist also leads an active social life, in which he often finds opportunities to talk with members of Congress.

Both the bureaucrats and the lobbyists are regarded with some suspicion, but much of their testimony contains useful and honest information selected, of course, for the benefit of the cause that the witness is serving. Some of the most important information collected by the committees is purely political—who wants the bill passed and who wants it blocked, and which side has the most political weight?

Few members of Congress have time to become experts on any subject other than politics itself, and as the tasks of government have become more complicated, Congress has come to admit the need for expert guidance of its own. Most of the committees have staffs including one or more experts. There is an Office of Legislative Counsel in each house that drafts bills for the committees and individual members, with due regard to the mass of existing laws into which every new law must be correctly fitted.

In recent years Congress has considerably enlarged the Legislative Reference Service in the Library of Congress. This service is made up of experts on many subjects who are expected to report the pertinent facts without political prejudice. Some of the members of Congress use this service constantly to dig up facts for their speeches or for use in committee work.

Any description of how Congress works must give the impression that it can not come out with any sensible result, and yet it often does what the occasion requires and what the people want. Since 1933 the number of world-shaking decisions that Congress has had to make in every session has constantly increased. It would seem impossible that the intelligent and patriotic men in Congress, heavily overworked as they are, could have mastered these great problems. Yet the new legislation, all the way from the first years of the New Deal to the Marshall Plan and the new defense program, has shown a high percentage of success and of bipartisan acceptance over the course of the years. Something guides the Congress. It seems fair to say that the principal guiding force is the system of politics by which the American people express their needs, their desires, and their judgments. Congress, with all the seeming confusion of its working methods, is a sensitive instrument for translating the will of the people into the acts of government.

But the inefficiency of Congress is constantly criticized, and at rather long intervals Congress itself is hounded into a spasm of reform. The latest such spasm was in 1946, after a study by the American Political Science Association had been taken up by a special joint committee under Senator LaFollette and Congressman Monroney. The reorganization of 1946 not only reduced the number of committees; it also strengthened the technical staffs, raised the members' salaries, and relieved Congress of the galling job of settling small claims against the Government by passing a separate bill for each one. But the reorganization has been criticized because it did not cover all the needed reforms and yet did use up the opportunity, which may not soon come again.

The seniority system is cordially hated, especially by liberals, since the oldest men in both parties are apt to be conservative. These older men get the seats of power, and occasionally a rather glaring case of dotage is seen at the head of an important committee.

The principal argument for keeping the seniority system is that it settles most of the problems of choice while Congress is being organized. While organizing, the majority party must stand together, for it may have only a slim margin of votes. If the party were to split over the choice of a chairman for a strategic committee such as Ways and Means, the minority party would in effect choose between the candidates. There seems to be little prospect that the practical politicians who control the rules of the Senate and House will reform the seniority custom.

Another custom that has long been a target for criticism is the filibuster in the Senate. When a small but determined group of senators will not accept a bill, they can talk it to death, by speaking in relays for an indefinite period. They do not need to discuss the subject; it is within the Senate rules to read aloud from Shakespeare or a cookbook.

The Senate has a "cloture" rule, under which it can limit debate by a two-thirds vote. The rule has been carefully designed to be almost unworkable, because neither party actually wants to give up the right to filibuster.

The filibuster is criticized on the ground that it violates the principle of majority rule. No one, of course, would use the filibuster against a bill unless the majority were prepared to vote for it. On the other hand, there is a deep-seated feeling in the Senate that the Federal principle does not warrant absolute majority rule on proposals that seem unendurable to a minority of the States. There has always been a strong feeling among the American people that majority rule has its limits, and especially that no majority has a right to rule except where it is a majority. South Carolina feels that it should not be ruled by a majority of New Yorkers. It should be kept in mind, too, that the Senate itself was designed to be a contradiction to the popular majority principle of the House. In the Senate each State has two votes regardless of how many voters it has; and this arrangement was invented for the exact purpose of protecting the smaller States from being outvoted by the larger ones. It is not surprising, therefore, that in the tradition of the Senate a minority that is prepared to go to great lengths to escape some proposed control that it regards as oppressive should be given more respect than its mere numbers would seem to warrant. There is, therefore, small chance that a simple and easy rule for limiting debate, such as is found in the House, will ever be acceptable to the Senate.

A number of proposed reforms are aimed at improving the working efficiency of the Senate and House, which is low by any ordinary standard of management. One proposal is that the two houses install electric voting boards, like those now in use in some State legislatures. The time that it takes to call the roll is a serious waste, especially in the House; and the roll-call periods are of little use for incidental work, such as conferring with other members on the floor. With the electric system all the members would vote at the same time and the board would show the score immediately and keep the record.

Another proposal is to give home rule to the District of Columbia. At present, Congress is the Board of Aldermen of the District, and also its county government and State legislature, as well as the Federal legislature over all. Washingtonians, however, cannot vote unless they maintain a residence outside the District and vote there.

Both Senate and House have District committees. Congress passes the local tax laws, decides whether to widen 20th Street and how the barbershops shall be inspected. Such jobs seem out of scale for the legislature that has to decide the measure of American co-operation with the United Nations or the North Atlantic Treaty Organization.

When local self-government in the District was abolished in 1878, the purpose was reform. In those days city government in the United States had sunk to depths of corruption that are not often plumbed by any city at the present time. Those who propose relieving the congressmen of the petty job of running the District point out that with modern methods a city can be honestly and efficiently operated by its own government.

The most conspicuous cause of lost motion and distraction in Congress is the stream of tourists from home. Americans like to visit the nation's capital, and they like to have their congressman buy them a lunch in the House restaurant, get them tickets for the theater, and find them a hotel room. The high-school basketball team wants the senator to get the President to stand with the team on the White House steps for a photograph. This, by the way, refers to a true story, and when one senator sternly reminded the boys that the President was running a war, the other senator was glad to get an advantage over his colleague by promptly taking the matter up with the White House.

No one has ventured to propose any way of telling the constituents to leave their representative alone, lest they pointedly leave him alone in the next election. In fact, the congressmen regard constant contact with the home folks as so valuable that when Congress is not in session they usually go home to see more of the folks. The most practicable means for handling this growing flood of visitors would seem to be merely to hire more staff to take over the routine work, so the congressmen can have time for visiting. Any congressman who cannot enjoy the art of deciding how to vote while walking through the tunnel from his office to the House with two constituents talking into each ear is likely to die or resign, leaving the job to someone with a more durable nervous system.

The fact seems to be that the reason the Congress works in a steady uproar, as it does, and at the same time accomplishes so much of what the people want done, is that this is the natural politician's way of working. The politician represents the human race as it is found in his home territory, raised to a more than usual horsepower. The noise he makes is the American noise, a shocking sound to foreigners who have noises of their own at home. But such as we are, the American people have managed to face without utter disaster dangers and problems that the fathers of the Constitution never knew. There seems to be some hope that the United States may come through with a success that will not only be gratifying to Americans but helpful to other free peoples. The American Congress has a full set of the faults and virtues of the people it represents, and in the long run comes out with about the same degree of successful work.

VII.
FEDERAL COURTS

THE FEDERAL COURTS, AND THE REGULATING AGENCIES that act somewhat like courts, apply the law to particular cases; but they do far more than that. For the words of the written law cannot be all the law. New cases arise, and the law must deal with them. Sometimes Congress passes new laws to deal with new cases. But sometimes the courts find new meanings in the old laws, which the courts declare to be in line with the true spirit of the old law.

Which kind of adjustment will be taken is a political decision depending mainly on the personal attitudes of the judges, and especially on the attitudes of the members of the Supreme Court. These men are not detached from the political system, since they were appointed by a man who had won the Presidency, and since even in the seclusion of the highest Court, they feel the moral standards and the political judgments of their fellow countrymen.

The problem of what ought to be done when the Government violates the Constitution was not directly faced in the first days of the Republic. The Constitution was adopted as the "supreme law of the land," and any act of Congress or of the President that violates it is in theory not a law. As James Bryce said in 1896, "Such acts as they do in excess of their powers are void, and may be, indeed ought to be, treated as void by the meanest citizen." Bryce considered that the authority of the Supreme Court to declare a law unconstitutional was logical and unassailable. Historically, however, that authority has been assailed by experts, including Andrew Jackson and Abraham Lincoln. It was hotly questioned during the Court-packing controversy in 1937.

In the colonial governments, where the basic law was a royal charter, the courts sometimes held a law to be void as a violation of the charter. The States carried on the tradition. In 1786 a law passed by the legislature of Rhode

Island was held void by the State Supreme Court on the ground that it violated the State constitution.

Thus in 1803, when Chief Justice John Marshall wrote the first Supreme Court opinion declaring an act of Congress void, he was assuming a power which had a traditional logic that he took to be a solid basis for action. He said that the principle that an act contrary to the Constitution is void "is essentially attached to written constitutions, and is consequently to be considered, by this court, as one of the fundamental principles of our society."

During the next fifty years, another theory of how to deal with violations was proposed—the theory that any State had a right to nullify a Federal law that it regarded as unconstitutional or unacceptable. In 1828 John C. Calhoun prepared a paper for the legislature of South Carolina, afterward called the "South Carolina Exposition," in which he stated that constitutionally the Federal Government was only the agent of the States. He asserted that any State could nullify a Federal law if it found itself displeased by the actions of Congress, and that it could then forbid the enforcement of that law in the State. The law was then "unconstitutional" and could be made binding only by an amendment to the Constitution, voted by three-fourths of the States.

Fortified by Calhoun's reasoning, hotheads in South Carolina proposed to nullify a Federal tariff law. President Jackson replied that the Union must be preserved and he would enforce the law with troops if necessary. This issue was compromised by an act of Congress softening the law.

Twenty years later the Wisconsin legislature refused to recognize the Federal law that required a Northern State to return a fugitive slave found in its territory. This method of voiding Federal laws that a State might consider oppressive was found to lead to civil war, and the War of 1861–1865 wiped out nullification for good. Meanwhile the Supreme Court had quietly continued to judge laws on the basis of their conformity to the Constitution, although after 1803 it did not declare any Federal laws unconstitutional until 1857. But after the Civil War the amount of positive legislation increased and the Court began to use its power more often.

In the course of time, the people have gotten used to the

Federal Courts

fact that when the Court strikes down a law that is widely popular, the meaning of this setback is simply that the people used the wrong instrument. In effect the Court says: "You did not give Congress the authority in 1787 to levy income taxes. If you want income taxes now [in 1895], you cannot get them by asking Congress. Ask yourselves instead, by way of an amendment to your Constitution." So the people went back and started over, deciding this time whether they wanted income taxes enough to put through a Constitutional amendment. In 1913 they decided, and the Sixteenth Amendment, directly permitting income taxes, was adopted. The fact that the Supreme Court can be overruled by the long and patient process of amending the Constitution is well known; but it does not necessarily satisfy the people when they are in an impatient mood.

The Supreme Court is made up of lawyers who had long and successful experience before they were appointed to the Court. Not all were judges or lawyers in private practice. A Supreme Court justice may have been a senator, an attorney general, a teacher in a law school, or even the administrator of an agency that acts like a court. The typical justice was probably appointed at about the age of fifty, and will live from twenty to forty years on the Court. He is therefore likely to be somewhat elderly, and also to have lived in close contact with the political world of the previous generation. The Court has often been conservative in its opinions, and therefore galling to liberals who wanted rapid progress. In 1937, the Court happened to be unusually old, and the party in power was moving too fast for the Court. The result was the famous "Court-packing plan."

Between 1935 and 1937 many of the New Deal laws came before the Court and were declared unconstitutional. President Roosevelt said that the justices were too old and proposed to Congress that the nine justices be supplemented by enlarging the Court to possibly fifteen members. This "packing" scheme offended so many people that it was rejected by Congress; but the Court shifted its ground enough to get out of the way before the President could try some other line of attack. After 1937, resignations and deaths allowed Mr. Roosevelt to name eight new justices. The Court made practically no further objections to the

Government's program during the remainder of the twenty years of Democratic rule.

The inferior courts in the Federal system have somewhat less political importance, since their principal duty is to settle routine cases where no constitutional question is at stake. At the ground level are the district courts, with about two hundred district judges scattered over the United States. These courts handle both civil and criminal cases that come under the jurisdiction of the Federal laws. By the Constitution they are required to give a jury trial in all except civil cases involving less than twenty dollars.

Civil cases coming into the district court include those where a citizen sues for his rights under a Federal law such as the Employers' Liability Act, which requires an employer engaged in interstate commerce to compensate an employee who is injured in course of his work. The district court also handles cases arising on the high seas, since the Constitution places admiralty law under the Federal Government. A third type of case is a dispute between citizens of different States. This may include almost any business dispute, since a corporation is a citizen of the State where it is chartered and may operate in all the other States, where it is legally an outsider.

Criminal cases in the district courts are based on charges of a violation of Federal law, such as the antitrust laws or wartime price controls, or the laws against smuggling and kidnaping. In tax cases the Government may be prosecuting a citizen for tax frauds, or a citizen may be suing the Government for taxes he claims were not rightfully due.

The district courts have "original jurisdiction" in nearly all cases. That is, they collect the facts, usually with a jury. The parties may appeal the decision either on the ground that the court made an error in conducting the trial, or on the ground that the law is unconstitutional. The appeals go up to the middle layer of Federal courts, the circuit courts of appeals.

A court of appeals accepts the facts sent up to it by the lower court, and therefore does not need a jury. Its work is to decide on disputed questions of law. As a rule the court of appeals sits with three judges together on the bench. This court's principal duty is to protect the Supreme Court from routine cases of no political importance. Even when the appeal claims that a law is unconstitutional, the court of appeals can hear the arguments and often can clarify the points that are actually in dispute. Its decision may be so clear and well grounded that the Supreme Court will refuse to go into the question further, in which case the court of appeals has stated the supreme law of the land, at least for the exact circumstances of that case.

But if two cases that seem to be almost the same are decided in opposite ways by two courts of appeals, or if the Supreme Court wants to overrule or to expand the opinion of the appeals court, the Supreme Court will accept an appeal. In addition there are some kinds of business law, especially in antitrust cases and certain cases of regulation, that are of such political importance and so complicated in their details that Congress has decided to shorten their slow progress through the Federal courts. Such cases may begin in a lower court composed of three district judges who collect the facts and give a decision that can be directly appealed to the Supreme Court without being combed over by the court of appeals.

Outside the three-layer Federal court system there are a number of special courts, such as the Court of Claims, the Tax Court, and the Court of Customs and Patent Appeals. The special courts have been established to handle subjects that are difficult for a judge to understand unless he devotes his whole time to this one type of problem. The special courts are on a border line between strictly "judicial" courts and the administrative agencies with practically judicial powers, through which the Government regulates certain kinds of business.

Government regulation of business, as we now have it, was not one of the purposes of the original Constitution, although the commerce clause gives Congress the power "to regulate Commerce with foreign Nations and among the several States, and with the Indian Tribes." That kind of regulation would consist mainly of tariffs and embargoes, and in particular of prohibiting state tariffs and embargoes. But as business grew more complicated, Congress had to regulate such matters as railroad rates, safety of travel, the adulteration of food and drugs, and the allocation of radio channels. The peculiar feature of these latter types of regulation is that Congress cannot know or pass upon the facts in each case. The railroad freight charge on oranges in crates from Silver Springs, Florida, to Syracuse, New York, cannot be made an act of Congress. Yet there are more or less definite principles of fairness and of a sound relation between different rates which Congress wants to see applied. Congress can pass a law stating these principles in a general way. From there on someone must be hired to study the facts and make a decision on the basis of the principles laid down in the law.

Among the principal regulatory agencies are the Interstate Commerce Commission, which supervises the rates on interstate transportation; the Federal Trade Commission, handling antitrust law violations and some kinds of sharp practice such as dishonest advertising; the Federal Communications Commission; the Federal Power Commission; and the Securities and Exchange Commission.

As a rule the commission, after finding the facts, will either tell the business concern what it can charge for its services, or what change in its practices it must adopt in order to comply with the law. The regulatory agencies do not have power to collect fines or put anyone in jail. But to back up their orders they have the power to take the businessman to court and accuse him of defying the law. That is, these agencies make the law, so far as the individual example is concerned. They make the law in a much greater degree than any Federal courts except the Supreme Court itself.

The courts do not like to admit that law can be made by an administrative agency which does not quite fit into the standard picture of a three-part government. The administrative agency is a cross between the executive and the judicial, with a strong flavor of legislative. It is influenced by politics, since the commissions are chosen by the President and thoroughly examined by the Senate. It is not uncommon for the business concerns that are to be regulated to contribute generously to the party funds, and more than one commissioner has been rejected by the Senate because he stood up for the public interest against a powerful industry. The old proverb about who is going to watch the watchman has often an answer that is more political than the courts think proper.

The courts, however, have not been without some power

Federal Courts

to watch the regulating agencies. They do not want so much to question the facts reported by the agency as to supervise its methods of collecting facts and of coming to conclusions. Within limits they are willing to allow rougher methods than they would allow to the police. The Supreme Court decided in 1950 that the Federal Trade Commission could properly go into the Morton Salt Company and look through the files just to make sure whether the law was being obeyed. Such a "fishing expedition" would not be proper for a court or for ordinary police. The definition of "due process of law" is gradually being remodeled to fit the special needs of government regulation.

The Government is often a party to actions in the Federal courts. The first Attorney General was appointed in 1789 to argue government cases before the Supreme Court. In the present-day Department of Justice the Solicitor General is now in charge of this work. The department acts as the Government's lawyer. If the Internal Revenue Bureau is convinced that a man has evaded his income taxes, it turns the case over to the Department of Justice for prosecution. If a Senate Committee cannot get a witness to answer questions, or if it believes the witness has lied, the department is called upon to present the case to a grand jury and see if it can get an indictment for contempt or perjury.

The Department of Justice also includes the Federal Bureau of Investigation, the most important of the Federal detective services. The FBI deals with kidnapers, bank robbers, and many other violators of Federal law, and is active in counterespionage. It does the field work of investigating the loyalty of Government employees. Other secret services, located in the Treasury, pursue counterfeiters, smugglers, narcotics traders, income-tax dodgers, and persons who threaten the life of the President. All such persons when caught are prosecuted in Federal courts by the Department of Justice or the local United States attorneys under its supervision.

The Department of Justice cannot hope to prosecute every violation of law that comes to its attention, especially the borderline cases where only a long court action will show whether the law was violated at all. In antitrust policy, for instance, the Attorney General has to decide what cases are likely to bring out legal questions for decision that will develop the law in the ways that he thinks desirable. Cases of undeniable defiance of the law are comparatively rare; the usual situation is one where legal experts differ.

Accordingly, the Attorney General has a wide discretion about what laws to enforce and about what actions he will regard as violations of the law. His decisions will not be made without reference to the policies of the President; and these in turn are strongly influenced by politics.

For example, when the Truman Administration turned over the Department of Justice to President Eisenhower, several great antitrust cases were on the way to the courts. One, against U.S. Steel, raised a fundamental question of the kind of subsidiary companies that a great raw-material producer could properly control. President Eisenhower could not avoid deciding whether his Attorney General would best bring such a question before the courts or drop it.

With all the political forces that influence the interpretation of the Constitution and the laws, from the choices of the Attorney General to the personalities of the Supreme Court justices, the law is evidently not the simple block of enduring granite that the layman might wish he could have under his feet. The law, in fact, is less certain today than it was thought to be in 1787. In those days the prevailing belief was that underlying human laws there was a "natural law" which God had ordained and which learned judges could discover and declare. Blackstone's famous *Commentaries* were founded on this theory, and they strongly influenced American lawyers and judges in the early days of the Republic.

But even in 1776 Jeremy Bentham, who had studied under Blackstone at Oxford, began a revolt against his doctrine. Bentham looked at the London slums and said that God's law did not seem to him to be directing the laws of England. He said that men could make laws to serve a useful purpose, such as getting rid of slums. This was called the "utilitarian" theory. It led straight on into the later American philosophy of "pragmatism"—meaning that if a thing works it must be correct. This change has revolutionized the political attitude of the American people

Federal Courts

toward law, and in due time has even moved the attitude of legal experts and judges.

So long as the law was supposed to be already established in God's mind and not to be found except in the Bible and in the studies of learned jurists, the people at least believed it to be a solid mountain where Moses could find solid stone tablets, up there in the mist. But now that the law is supposed to be an instrument that men use to bring order and justice and even prosperity, it is something quite different. Instead of a simple, cloud-capped mountain, we now range over a whole landscape, where high-powered steam shovels are constantly at work moving some of the mountains—but not all. We have to understand which mountains move and which do not. The simple, though often cruel, certainties of the legal pundits of a hundred and fifty years ago are being replaced by more practical but complicated efforts to make the world the way we want it. And making the world to suit the sovereign people is largely a matter of politics.

The new Supreme Court set up by the Democrats since 1937 has not found as sure a footing among the questions of the modern "positivist" state as the earlier Courts believed they had in the older theories of law. For if the law itself is not a certainty, where are the standards of judgment?

The principles of right and decency, of justice and good will, have not ceased to operate because we no longer believe that learned judges can draw knowledge of them from a special inspiration. The people still have principles of judgment, and it is those principles that judges, since they, too, are people, are asked to interpret. The effect is that nearly every Supreme Court decision is accompanied by several separate opinions giving different reasons for agreeing or dissenting. But the process of seeking for whatever of solid truth may be found to stand upon has not ceased.

VIII.

THE STATES

THE STATES HAVE ALL THE ORDINARY RIGHTS AND POWERS of independent nations except:

1) rights forbidden to the States by the Federal Constitution;

2) rights allowed to both the States and the Federal Government, insofar as Federal use of these rights may conflict with State use of the same rights;

3) the right of secession, or resigning from the Union.

For example, the Constitution forbids the States negotiating with a foreign government. A State may negotiate with another State, but any treaty between the States—called an "interstate compact"—will be legal only after Congress approves it.

Both State and Federal governments can regulate business and labor practices connected with interstate commerce, and there is constant litigation to define the border line between their proper fields of authority.

In their internal affairs, the States are independent, even in matters that will affect other States by competition, such as state income tax and divorce laws. A State can go far in making itself a nuisance to other States before an amendment or a new interpretation of the Federal Constitution can be found to stop it.

A new State is admitted only after Congress approves its proposed constitution as giving it "a republican form of government." But once admitted, it has all the original sovereign powers of one of the thirteen original States. Thereafter Congress cannot change a State constitution except indirectly, by suggesting an amendment to the Federal Constitution.

For example, in the original Constitution the States reserved the power to decide who would have the right to vote. In voting for congressmen, the Constitution accepted whatever qualifications each State had laid down for those

The States

who could vote for members of its lower house. The Federal Congress had no authority to change the rules set up by State constitutions and State laws; but it could propose amendments to the Federal Constitution by which three-quarters of the States could override the remainder.

It was by such amendments, for example, that the States were forced to give women the vote and to choose their United States senators by popular vote.

In the Fourteenth Amendment, adopted in 1868, the Northern States attempted to force the Southern States to allow Negroes to vote. This amendment has not been strictly enforced because political pressures have not allowed Congress to cut down the number of Representatives from such States, as the amendment provides. But social and economic progress in the South, together with Supreme Court decisions that were not resisted or evaded, have gradually brought the Negroes in most Southern States the right to vote in the Democratic primaries. This is the real crux of the question. It could be said that the Democratic party, not being named in the Constitution, was a private organization with a right to pick its own membership; and yet the real choice of the men who would be elected in the legal election was made in the Democratic primaries. The gradual solution of this problem was beyond the practical scope of legal powers; it had to await the development of public opinion that would make a solution politically acceptable to the South.

The State has the sole power to charter local governments, in the same way that the British Parliament might charter, combine, or even abolish the governments of London. There is often a conflict between the State and a big city, such as New York or Chicago, with a budget larger than the State budget. The city cannot change its own form of government or decide whether to operate its own local underground transit system without getting permission from the State legislature.

There is a tendency for the legislature to divide the State into assembly districts in such a way as to give more seats to the farmers than to the city people. Moreover, in the politically "doubtful" States, the city government is apt to be Democratic, and the State legislature Republican.

The State governor commands the State police and the

militia. These forces must not be sent against another State, but can be used to keep internal order. The militia can be called into Federal service, and on the other hand the governor can call on the U.S. Army for help if he is unable to suppress disorder. The governor is in charge of enforcing some but not all of the laws. He is the man who deals with the Federal Government; and he attends governors' conferences where he discusses problems and politics with his peers. The governor has the power of pardon, sometimes restricted by the advice of a parole or pardon board.

Unlike the President of the United States, the governor of a State is usually surrounded by lesser executive officers who were elected by the people and do not depend on him for their jobs. The lieutenant governor, who is the heir, may be at odds with the governor, and a deadlock inside the State administration is not unknown.

A peculiarity of the executive system in some states is the "recall." By petition the people may call a special election to vote on the removal of a governor or other officers. This procedure theoretically allows the voters to settle a deadlocked quarrel among their elected officials; but it has perhaps been more useful as a warning than as a means of making peace after a war has broken out in the Statehouse.

Another difference between governor and President is that the governor is in a position to aspire to a higher office, and often does so. When a United States senator dies, the governor of his State may resign and let the lieutenant governor appoint him to the Senate. But as a rule he will appoint a friend or a rival to the job; and these appointments are not always guileless. Much may depend on who will next be running for the Senate, and whether the governor wants to go to the Senate at that opportunity or to be re-elected as governor for the time being. In the most important doubtful States, such as New York or Ohio, the governor is apt to have an eye on the White House. His maneuvers between State capitol and United States Senate may be well-timed jockeying for the starting line of a future national convention of his party.

The State legislature is the orphan of American politics, being neither glamorous enough to attract public attention like the United States Congress, nor close enough to home to arouse local reform movements as city governments often have done.

The people of the States have traditionally regarded their State legislatures as part-time assemblies. The members were merely influential private citizens, meeting for a few weeks every year or every second year to settle the problems of the State. The pay, therefore, has been regarded as a fee to compensate for time lost, rather than as a full-time salary. It is not surprising, therefore, that many legislators carry on private businesses or law offices in their home towns. Sometimes the legislator's private work may affect his judgment on public matters that he is called upon to decide.

In one State, for example, the State senators before World War II were being paid less than $700 a year. The representative of an outside corporation with large mineral interests in the State was quoted as boasting that no "severance tax" could be imposed on his company because a majority of the senators were retained as lawyers for his company in their home districts, at a fee of $5,000 a year.

In many States there are one or more State bosses who represent the most powerful business interests. State legislation is important to many kinds of business. It is important to contractors who want to build public works and to gamblers who do not want to be regulated or closed down. The boss may handle such questions to the satisfaction of his customers through a system of controls in the legislature. His power rests on a well-founded belief that he can cause the defeat of any member of the legislature who refuses to take his advice.

On the other hand, some legislators eke out their salaries by introducing "shakedown" bills. A member may propose an extravagant fire-protection law for theaters, or a law for the regulation of loan sharks that might be desirable if he had any intention of getting it passed. The frightened theater owners or loan sharks are advised to hire a certain lawyer to reason with the legislator; and upon payment of a bribe disguised as a legal fee, the bill is allowed to die.

The comparatively low moral standards of State government seem to be the result of lack of political interest among the voters. The people seldom know or care about the complexities of State law and its relation to business. They do not want to pay honest men enough to allow them to serve the State with no private business of their own. They do not pay enough attention to State politics to give an honest man a chance to muster their votes in the face of a well-oiled party machine. But from time to time a scandal rouses the people to demand reforms.

Because of the people's distrust of the State legislature, one kind of reform, the initiative and referendum, was adopted by about twenty States as part of their constitutions around the year 1900. The people can "initiate" a law by presenting a petition signed by about 10 per cent of the voters; or they can start a "referendum" to block a measure that is up for action in the legislature. The petition forces a special election in which the voters pass or reject the law over the legislature's head. This direct form of democracy is so cumbrous that it has not been as much used as its inventors hoped in 1900, but it stands as a stick behind the door in case the legislature gets into a scandal that arouses the public.

Another result of distrust of the legislature is a tendency for the States to put legislation into their constitutions. The effect has been to make some of the State constitutions excessively long and to reduce their dignity as the supreme law of the State.

In view of the handicaps of lack of public interest and dignity, it is remarkable that so much of the active political progress of the American people has been made by the use of State powers. The people often prevail when they focus their attention, or when an able governor draws attention to what the people want done.

The States have pioneered in many lines of progress, such as regulation of railroads, public utilities, and the liquor business. They passed the first American labor laws to protect women and children. They have authorized cities to experiment with new forms of city government. In recent years, the State legislatures have shown an interest in self-improvement, setting up legislative research services, bill-drafting offices, and interstate associations for the study of legislative problems.

In fact, much of the general welfare legislation of the Federal Government has grown out of State legislation, in the same way that the commerce clause originally grew out of the confusion of State regulation of business. Federal social security laws, for instance, are the offspring of State laws. One of the strong reasons for the Federal laws was to give every American a definite set of rights even if he moved from one State to another, as so many millions do. The States continue to be laboratories in which new laws are tried. If these experiments succeed, the experience of the States guides the popular decision whether to continue the law, and whether it belongs in the State or the Federal system.

The State courts are set up in a system that looks like the system of Federal courts, with a supreme court at the top that has the power to declare State laws unconstitutional. The State courts, however, are much closer to the people and deal with a different kind of law. Whereas the Federal courts speak mainly of what they find in the Federal Constitution, the State courts rest upon all the law there is, except what has been delegated to the Federal Government. Some of the State law is found in the State constitution and the statutes passed by the legislature. But a large part of it is the common law of England, inherited and adapted by court decisions to the conditions and moral judgments of the American people. In Louisiana much of the inherited law is French, brought down from the Code Napoléon.

The common law is made up of the record of past decisions, including those of the British courts, and covers all the ordinary crimes and disputes between citizens, except where the legislature has taken over and substituted a statute law. The "due process" which is guaranteed to all Americans under the Constitution is very nearly the same as "due observance of the common law."

For example, in 1876 an Illinois law regulating warehouses, which had been upheld by the courts in Illinois, was taken to the United States Supreme Court on the plea that it took property without due process of law. The Court decided that the warehouses could be regulated because they were "affected with a public interest." The Court based this definition of due process on the English common law "from whence came the right that the Constitution respects." Even the Federal Government, resting purely on its own Constitution, is governed by the common law wherever it has not been changed by legislation or constitutional amendment.

The State courts deal more often with cases in "equity" than do the Federal courts. Equity is a separate set of principles, applying only to civil disputes, such as how to divide an estate among the heirs. Equity determines whether the judge will issue an injunction against a man who is about to take some action, legal in itself, that will injure some other person without just cause.

Equity was developed in England because the people were dissatisfied with the common law, which was too rigid to do justice in unusual situations. Equity represented the "conscience of the king," whose prerogative allowed him to reach down and correct a palpable injustice in the machinery of the law. The king's conscience was kept by the Chancellor, and the Chancery Court developed a separate system of principles, including rules derived from church law and the Roman law.

In England, as readers of Charles Dickens remember, the Court of Chancery had become so entangled in its own processes that the heirs of large estates did not quickly obtain settlements. In the United States, the inherited rules of equity have been limited and regulated by legislation. Some States have separate chancery courts to try equity cases; but most State courts and all Federal courts deal in both law and equity.

In most of the States the lowest courts are the magistrates' or police courts, where the judge or magistrate can send a drunk to jail for thirty days, or fine a motorist for speeding, without the aid of a jury. He may also have authority to receive a man accused of murder and decide whether to hold him for trial in a higher court.

Above the magistrates' courts are the regular trial courts, which try cases of sufficient importance to require the attention of a jury.

The dirty politics in the courts can usually be found in the magistrates' or the police courts, where the man on the bench has often had no legal training and owes his appointment to the shadier type of political influence. Corruption in the trial courts is much less frequent.

In most States the judges of the trial courts are elected

The States

by the people for limited terms. The lawyers do not like the election of judges, on the ground that the judge has to follow the political weather too closely. Bar associations try to influence the nominations so as to get good judges, as looked at from their point of view. Labor unions and farm organizations defend the popular election of judges because they fear that the governor or the legislature would choose judges with a bias in favor of Big Business. Thus the State trial courts, where most of the litigation of the American people is carried on, are inevitably forced to respect the political forces operating in the State. They therefore tend to represent that standard of honesty and justice that the voters will effectively support or demand.

State administrations have usually contained more employees appointed by political pull and fewer under the merit system than the Federal administrative branch. Like the legislatures, the State civil services have suffered from public neglect. But there have been several forces pushing toward improvement.

One of these forces is the great increase in technical public services, such as health protection and engineering, where the common political hanger-on would be so ineffective as to attract public criticism of the party in power. These services require the adoption of a merit system, which then tends to spread.

Another influence is Federal aid, which at first offers a lush field for graft and mismanagement by the State officials who have the local responsibility for using the money. A short experience of this sort of behavior serves to arouse the people. The party in power in Washington finds that it is getting no credit for its help to the States. The next appropriation will carry a requirement that the State must adopt a merit system for the administration of the Federal funds.

With such forces helping to bring honest and competent people into State administrations, the usual civic organizations that press for better government at the State capital are aided and encouraged.

Most of the State governments have trouble meeting expenses out of their own revenues, not because their budgets are large in comparison with other American enterprises, but because they are in a poor position to collect taxes. A state budget for an agricultural State may run between one hundred and two hundred million dollars; for a State like New York it will be closer to one billion, comparable to the budgets of medium to large business corporations in the United States. New York State's budget is smaller than that of New York City.

A State government can collect taxes on real estate, movable property, licenses to do business, sales or transactions, business or personal incomes, and excises such as the gasoline and cigarette taxes. Property taxes are limited by the fact that they are an important source of local revenues, and the total tax on a piece of property must not rise too high or the owner will abandon it. Income taxes are limited by the fact that the Federal Government collects a heavy income tax, especially in the upper brackets. A rich man who has to pay 60 or 75 per cent of his income to the Federal Government cannot well pay the State a similar per cent of what he has left.

State income taxes therefore cannot make as wide a difference between low and high bracket rates as the Federal tax can impose. Since the property and sales taxes, and the gasoline and tobacco taxes as well, rest more heavily on the low incomes than on the high, the general tendency of State taxation is depressing to business. Any undue effort of a State to raise its tax rates immediately starts a flow of business over the border if things can be bought more cheaply in an adjoining State.

Because of the limitations on revenue, the State responsibilities are limited and there is a tendency for the State to rest some of the load on the Federal Government. States expect several important kinds of help from the Federal Treasury. Road and school subsidies are old in the American tradition. Since 1933 many of the State responsibilities for relief of unemployment and other forms of distress have been taken over by the Federal social security system. The principle of expanding Federal aid for public works in hard times is now generally accepted.

Federal aid to the States is based on two economic facts. One is that the Federal Government has greater tax-collecting power than the States, largely because no one can get away from the Federal Government except by moving out of the United States. The other is the fact that equalization is beneficial to the country as a whole. Some States are much richer than others. As a rule, investors in the richer States are in a position to draw income from business in the poorer States. If the Federal Government taxes the people of the richer States and pours some of the money back into the poorer States, the circulation does not dry up, and prosperity continues. The logic of equalization overcomes the simpler logic of State self-support.

In the same way, one of the chief responsibilities of a State government is to equalize a part of the inequality between the rich and poor parts of the State. The cities, as a rule, get the big end of the profit in trading with the farm country. Without interference, the farm properties gradually come into the possession of city banks, insurance companies, and investors, as indeed they did before 1933. The effect is bad for general prosperity. State subsidies to the poorest localities are required to correct the unbalanced results of private trade. These subsidies usually take the form of roads and other public works paid for by the State and of direct aid to schools and libraries and to local welfare funds.

The requirements of equalization, and the supremacy of the Federal taxing power, have caused the States to lift up their eyes to Washington, whence cometh their help. But this development worries the American people. The other side of the picture is the overgrowth of centralized bureaucracy in the Federal Government and its regional and local offices, with a corresponding loss of responsibility and dignity in the States. The leaders of both political parties have expressed the desire to find some way to limit the growth of Federal aid. Governor Stevenson, running in the campaign of 1952, emphasized the need for decentralizing responsibility as far as possible, from Washington to the States, and from the States to the local governments. President Eisenhower early in 1953 ordered a broad study of the relations between Federal and State revenues and responsibilities with a view to promoting a healthier political vitality in the States.

Several lines of action to build up the dignity and responsibility of the States have often been suggested. One is for the Federal Government to refrain from imposing certain kinds of taxes, such as the gasoline tax, which the

States depend upon for highway expenses. Another is a suggestion that the Federal Government collect certain taxes from the citizens of any State that neglects to levy those taxes, but not from anyone who is paying the tax to his own State. This form of pressure was used, for example, to bring States into co-operation with the Federal social security system, and its use has been suggested in connection with income taxation. State revenues can be considerably increased if no State is in a position to compete by offering easier terms to businesses or wealthy people moving into its territory.

Artificial devices of various kinds will probably be employed to counteract, as far as is politically feasible, the natural and powerful trend toward centralization. For the American people, although they often neglect their State governments, are strongly inclined to come to the rescue when the State seems to be in danger.

IX.
LOCAL GOVERNMENT

IN THE UNITED STATES MORE THAN HALF THE PEOPLE live in cities, and about a hundred of these cities have populations of more than one hundred thousand. Local government for the rest of the American people is supplied mainly by counties. There are also thousands of special districts for schools, sanitary services, and other purposes. The districts overlap counties, cities, and other districts. One citizen may pay taxes to half a dozen units of government, Federal, State, city, county, and a couple of districts.

Thomas Jefferson hated cities and regarded them as sinks of corruption. City political life in the United States was, in fact, notoriously corrupt during the nineteenth century, largely because the new people flocking in from Europe and from the American farms were an easy prey to the city political machines. Since 1900 there has been some improvement in the honesty and efficiency of city government. One cause of improvement in recent years has been the rising standard of living and social security of the city workers, cutting down somewhat on the need for charity and sympathy to which the political bosses had so skillfully catered. Another has been the adoption of more efficient forms of city government.

The cities have no sovereign rights of their own, but can usually exert some influence toward getting from the State the kind of charter that the citizens want. There are three forms of city government. The original form, with a mayor and council, is still the most common. The commission type of government first became famous in Galveston, Texas, where it was adopted in 1901 after a devastating flood as a device for handling the emergency. It spread rapidly to other medium-sized cities for about fifteen years, and then ceased to gain new adherents. Popular favor shifted toward the third type, the council-manager, or city-manager, plan, which is now operating in more than nine hundred cities of medium size.

In the old-fashioned mayor-and-council governments, the councilmen, or aldermen, were local politicians, and the city employees were appointed as a reward for political service. The corrupt city machines found the system well adapted to the lower forms of political manipulation, and were therefore generally opposed to the adoption of newer types of government. But many reforms have been put through in the mayor-and-council system itself.

Most of the councils have now been reduced from two chambers to one, and some of these single chambers have been reduced to a few members elected at large. City administrations have been reorganized as the cities have taken on more kinds of public services calling for more highly trained employees. Many cities have strengthened the powers of the mayor and given him more responsibility for managing the government, thus turning in the direction of the city-manager system, even when not actually adopting it.

The commission form of government was designed to give responsibility to a small group of men who would be conspicuous enough to get the benefit of full public attention. There are usually five members of the commission, one of whom acts as chairman and is called mayor. Policies are adopted by the commission as a whole, and each member takes charge of running a particular department. The chief weakness is that the commission can get into a deadlock and no one has power to untangle it.

In the council-manager system, first tried in Staunton, Virginia, in 1908, the council adopts the policies for the city and passes the city ordinances, but the administration is in the hands of a manager. The council hires the manager. He may come from another city; a successful manager therefore can hope to be called to a better job from time to time as he rises in the profession. The manager hires the city employees under a merit system that allows him enough leeway to do a good operating job.

The manager plan takes account of the plain fact that the work the people want the city government to do is much like the work of private business—producing and distributing services of the best quality at the lowest practical cost. The people therefore think it reasonable to set up a city corporation with a manager and board of directors, much like the ordinary private corporation, and with the people themselves taking the part of stockholders.

It is clear that a city can be run with less politics than a nation if the people want it that way because it has fewer problems of the kind that only politics can solve. It has no foreign relations, for example, and no fundamental economic problems like the national inflationary or deflationary policies that have to be decided in Washington. On the other hand, the manager system has been criticized by minorities that felt unprotected under a council elected at large and representing majority interests. Several cities have admitted the need of giving some recognition to the political differences among the people by allowing proportional representation in the council. Under this system, if a minority gets two-fifths of the votes, it gets two-fifths of the seats on the council, instead of none. Proportional representation in national elections would encourage the growth of splinter parties, and is therefore opposed as a danger to the two-party system. This general objection has limited the use of P.R. in cities.

The work of city governments has grown even faster than the cities themselves, because of the invention of new services that the citizens refuse to do without, and because the mere size and crowded condition of the cities cannot be endured without costly rapid transit and sanitation that were unnecessary in George Washington's day. Public works and utilities, fire prevention, schools and libraries, and police services grow more costly in proportion to the city's ability to raise revenue.

The chief sources of revenue are real estate and sales taxes, and direct taxes on business. But real estate and sales taxes also rest on business. If the city overloads its tax base it will drive business out to the suburbs beyond the range of the city's taxing power.

As a result of the gap between the revenues that the city can raise and the work it has to do to keep alive, most of the cities depend on subsidy. They depend on Federal subsidy because their States are dominated by the farmer vote and are engaged in equalizing operations, which mean taxing the city people and spreading the money over the farm country.

In New York in 1953 there was a dispute between the

mayor of New York City and the governor of the State over the amount of subsidy the City ought to receive from the State. The State was reported to be using 55 per cent of its tax revenues for aid to local governments. New York City's aid from the State amounted to 15 per cent of its own budget. The essence of the mayor's complaint was that the State laws contained allocation formulas that gave an unfair share of the aid funds to the smaller units.

The appeal of the cities to the Federal Government does not rest on the equalizing principle; for the most concentrated wealth is located in the big cities. It rests on the difference in power to tax. The city cannot lay heavy taxes on its rich men and rich corporations or they will move their offices away. But the Federal Government can tax them heavily and give some of the resulting money to the cities, and that is what it does.

The result is that ever since the cities broke down under the burden of relief in the Great Depression, there is a tendency for city governments to look upon their State government as a cruel stepmother and on the Federal Government as the generous uncle.

While many of the city services, especially the new and technical ones, have attained commendable standards of honesty and efficiency, the police in most cities have not done so well. They have a tradition of political appointments and political pull, reaching far back before the invention of merit systems. They have direct contact with organized crime, which will pay handsomely for protection. They are usually underpaid and treated with suspicion and disdain by the "good" people. In 1950 and 1951 a committee headed by U. S. Senator Estes Kefauver, investigating interstate crime, found evidence that city police forces were in the pay of the criminal organizations. It may be hoped that like other public services, the police will improve as growing technology in crime detection demands more highly trained men and as the police forces get more public attention and understanding.

For the sixty million Americans who do not live in cities the principal form of government is the county. The county has come down almost unchanged from Colonial times. It is governed by a board, usually of less than ten members, with a chairman who may also be the judge of the county court. The county keeps the records of property deeds, wills, marriages, and other private papers that require public record. The county builds local roads, conducts its local share in State and national elections, and is the unit for reporting the census and for drafting men into the armed forces. The county supplies the services of sheriff and coroner, courthouse and jail.

Counties in the different States have somewhat different kinds of work to do, different names for their officials, and all degrees of honesty and graft. These are the governments closest to the people and most deeply embedded in ancient traditions. Many county jobs are run by amateurs who work at it part time and often without pay. The country folk are conservative by habit and do not hasten to reform the methods handed down from their forefathers. Inefficiency and even graft are also among the ancient habits of the race.

The burden of paying for roads and schools has been shifting off the counties and onto the State and Federal treasuries, and even the local murder is likely to bring in the State detectives. The counties therefore have lost some of their traditional work by the progress of centralization. On the other hand, this same centralizing pressure has brought new jobs to the county government that previously had been performed by the smallest governmental unit, the local district.

Most districts are set up to operate a school. Others are tax districts, or road districts, or election districts that run a polling place on Election Day. Or a district may be simply the area served by a justice of the peace. Districts are apt to have only the simplest form of organization, if any. They are often reduced to mere ghosts as one-room schools are consolidated into centralized schools and other local jobs move into the county seat, following the building of paved roads and the increased use of automobiles.

In New England, towns were the original local units. The usual New England town covers thirty to sixty square miles and is about the area from which a farmer with horse and buggy could get to the courthouse and back in good weather. The basic element of government is the town meeting, where the citizens elect the selectmen to manage the town's affairs, and where they levy the taxes and decide whether to pave Quincy Street and buy benches for the park. This pure democracy works well until the population increases to an awkward size, when the town usually asks the State to incorporate it as a city.

Townships, usually six miles square, were established in some Northern States as a sort of cross between the town and the county. They have tended to be absorbed by the counties as hard roads have increased the ease of travel.

The coming of the automobile has had a disruptive effect on the traditional communities, the districts, villages, and neighborhoods where people visited, shopped, or went to church on foot or by horse travel. In the cities, people living in the same block are now apt to have jobs, friends, schools, and churches widely separated because of modern transportation. This development has undermined the social and political life commonly called the "grass roots." People can still learn politics and take part in party organization, but only by starting on a somewhat larger area than formerly and among larger numbers of strangers.

The American people are making efforts of various kinds to rearrange their customs and organizations to give them the feeling of belonging that has too often been lost with the breakup of the familiar neighborhood relationships. Even the U. S. Government tries to decentralize as many of its activities as possible. The Department of Agriculture has even experimented with artificial neighborhood groups organized to study a course of farm training, serving refreshments, and trying to bring families together as neighbors. The consolidated rural schools, the rural electrification co-operatives, and the State universities, all promote the revival of new and broader neighborhoods adjusted to the range of the automobile.

Although these new institutions are artificial inventions, they are no less American for that; Americans are often pleased to invent new institutions when they feel the need. The American people undoubtedly feel a deep distrust of the centralization that technical progress has been forcing upon them. They seek constantly for ways to decentralize, and to revive the grass roots from which their instinct tells them the vitamins of political life are derived. The gradual progress of the whole system of big and little government is being affected by the pressures of these centralizing and decentralizing forces in American life.

X.

GOVERNMENT AND BUSINESS

THE UNITED STATES, LIKE OTHER DEMOCRATIC COUNTRIES, has a mixed economic system. There is free competitive enterprise, much like the "capitalist" system described in the schoolbooks, covering most small business and manufacturing concerns, farmers, and independent professional men. There is Big Business operating under price leadership or other restraining influences, sometimes called "monopolistic competition." There are natural monopolies such as the telephone and domestic electric power services. There are co-operatives, in which the profits go to the customers rather than the stockholders. There are private non-profit institutions providing many kinds of services and supported partly or wholly by contributions—such as the churches, private universities, societies, clubs, philanthropic foundations, and labor unions. Then there are the government-owned enterprises, such as public schools and the Post Office.

The relations of government to business are complicated by the many different kinds of economic systems—each with its own needs and attitudes—including the government systems themselves, Federal, State, and local. Most of the pressures for government help have naturally come from the "capitalist" parts of the population, the big and small businessmen, bankers, and farmers, often in violent opposition to one another. But government aid has also been given to churches, colleges and co-operatives, mainly by tax exemption. Government regulation has affected the natural monopolies more than the other types of business.

The first purpose of setting up the Federal Government under the Constitution was the same as the purpose of the Schuman Plan in Europe—to help business by creating a big market area in place of many small ones separated by tariff walls. This the Federal Government accomplished by forbidding interstate trade barriers.

From there on, under the supervision of Alexander Hamilton, the Government proceeded to create a sound financial position, which necessarily was a help to business. The Government took responsibility for the almost worthless war bonds, including those of the States, which had been largely bought up by speculators for a few cents on the dollar. The Government taxed the people, mainly by tariffs on imports, and paid off the bonds. These payments helped to provide capital for starting new industries in the infant United States.

The tariff not only provided revenue, but was soon taken frankly as an instrument for raising the prices of foreign goods and so protecting new American industries from foreign competition.

The Federal Government started at an early date to give subsidies, direct and indirect, to private business. The Government helped out with the construction of canals and post roads, and later of the railroads. The Government gave away or sold for almost nothing most of the Western lands that it had bought or conquered. The virgin soil of the prairies and the virgin timber of Wisconsin and Minnesota were mined for many decades with no thought of conserving or restoring their original values. Until well into the twentieth century the prices of wheat and lumber did not have to cover the true cost, since the products were subsidized by eating up the capital value of field and forest. The Federal Government, during its first hundred years or more, was opening up new riches in the West and giving them to private business to be turned into money.

Policing of business developed more slowly. Business at first needed little Federal protection except from the ancient and well-known crimes of smuggling, counterfeiting, and piracy. In later years the growth of new industries and of far-flung and complicated trade gave birth to new abuses and to corresponding police duties.

The most important abuse that began to arouse the concern of the people in the second half of the nineteenth century was monopoly. Business after the Civil War of 1861–1865 became large enough to attract public attention to its monopolistic practices. The American people were still in a stage of active pioneering in which each family in the new Western States was largely independent in its daily life. But when the time came to sell the wheat and to buy supplies, the pioneer farmers found themselves in the grip of monopoly buyers, monopoly railway companies, and monopoly suppliers. They were outraged, and it is from this period that the peculiar American resistance to monopoly has been principally derived.

In the early 1890's the Populist party was formed among the farmers of the South and West to resist the encroachments of Big Business. This party demanded nationalization of railways and of the telegraph and telephone systems. The Populists called for a system of postal savings banks and a graduated income tax. They proposed to break the banks' monopoly of money by issuing "greenbacks," or paper money, and by "free coinage of silver." This latter proposal was inflationary in somewhat the same way as paper money because less than a dollar's worth of raw silver would be worth a dollar when stamped into a coin. Under William J. Bryan, the Democratic party took over the free-silver plank in 1896 and the Populists with it. Bryan lost the election.

But the popular indignation that broke out into the Populist movement had roused the two major parties by 1890 to do something on a national scale against monopoly. The result was the Sherman Antitrust Act. The Sherman Act declared all combinations or conspiracies in restraint of interstate or foreign trade to be illegal.

Before the passage of the Sherman Act the States had made some efforts to prevent monopolies by using the common law. These efforts became less and less effective as corporations grew larger and stretched their operations far across the country. The Sherman Act was drawn in general terms, much like a statement of the common law, or a Constitutional amendment. Its specific application has been defined by court decisions, supplemented occasionally by new legislation. In course of time, therefore, the antitrust law of the United States has taken on a common-law character of flexibility, as is necessary in attempting to control an evil that takes innumerable forms.

With all the ups and downs of antitrust-law enforcement, and all the glaring cases of large-scale restraint of trade, the

United States has unmistakably followed a different course from the usual European practice. The American people, whether Democrats or Republicans, give respect to the Sherman Act as one of the foundation stones of American freedom. Those who may be said to have violated the act have done so by interpretation, not in defiance of its sacred principle. Whatever hypocrisy may be involved is at least a wholesome deference to a basic theory of free competition that is deeply embedded in American thinking.

Whatever lapses from principle the American business world may exhibit, there is unquestionably a principle that distinguishes American thinking from that of most other free peoples. Americans believe cartels and monopolies to be morally wrong and economically suicidal. They believe that the antitrust law, tattered and shabby as it has sometimes appeared, has yet been a banner of freedom for independent men and therefore a major cause of American progress.

To the American people, the fact that the new European Coal and Steel Community has in its charter a strong antitrust law, designed to promote competition in order to improve the technical efficiency of the industries, is a gratifying example of progress in the right direction. The American people, by trial and error, have found that a "capitalist" system, as it grows richer and more productive, can be kept from the fatal diseases predicted by Karl Marx and his followers, but only through constant use of the government to weed it of monopoly growths.

Other less important kinds of police action have been established by Federal and State governments, mainly to protect consumers from being cheated. In simpler days when the farmers did all their business at the crossroads store, honesty was apt to be the best policy because the storekeeper had to live with his reputation. But as countrywide trade developed, and new, unknown products were offered for sale, the consumers got more and more out of their depth, and cheating of all kinds became more profitable. These conditions led to the passage of laws prohibiting use of dangerous poisons in cosmetics and foods and forbidding deceptive advertising claims. The law requires packaged foods and drugs to show the weight of net contents and a list of the materials used in making the product.

Government and Business

In a political sense laws against cheating are notable achievements; for the consumers are everybody and have almost no organized political power that they can focus on such a law. Producers are apt to be well organized and provided with strong lobbying agencies in Washington and in the State capitals. Sometimes the leaders of an industry may decide that strong protection of an honest product against the competition of adulterated brands will be more profitable than an unregulated market. In that case they may turn to and help to get protective laws. Often, however, such laws have been obtained by public pressure stirred up by newspaper or magazine articles and in the face of violent opposition from the industry.

One of the great struggles of the early part of President Franklin Roosevelt's Administration was the effort to enforce honesty in the securities markets. The Securities Act of 1933 and the Securities and Exchange Act of 1934 forced the corporations that issue stocks to make a true report on the condition of the company, on pain of responsibility for losses due to false claims. Another New Deal measure that affected the financial markets was the Holding Company Act of 1935, which was intended to prevent the piling up of public utility empires with tier upon tier of companies, each one owning the controlling stock of a series of companies in the next lower tier. These complicated empires had made it easy to shift the profits to the points where the manipulators of the system could absorb them, leaving the ordinary stockholders with nothing to show for their investment.

The financial companies that had been taking advantage of the public by false advertising, manipulation of the stock market, and the construction of fantastic holding companies fought the control laws bitterly. At one point a messenger boy, Elmer Danielson, testified that he had been hired to collect signatures at three cents each for telegrams opposing the Holding Company Act. There were also indications that country gravestones seemed to be telegraphing to Washington in great numbers, and always against the bill. Such evidences of dishonest opposition helped to get the financial acts through. The general effect was to reduce the hazards of the financial markets and increase public confidence; but at the time only the powerful political force of the victims of the depression made possible the passage of this legislation.

Another type of government relation with business is the work of supplying technical services, many of them free. Agricultural research and education services were among the first to be established in the Federal Government. The Federal Government now provides scientific research, statistical information, weather reports, and information on markets at home and abroad. The Government, as directed in the Constitution, gives patent and copyright protection.

Under President Herbert Hoover, the Reconstruction Finance Corporation was set up to lend money to corporations threatened with bankruptcy by the collapse of security values. This agency during World War II blossomed out into great operations such as the Metals Reserve Agency, Rubber Reserve Company, and Defense Supplies Corporation, lending and spending thousands of millions of dollars. In addition, the Export-Import Bank, set up in 1934, lends money to promote foreign trade. The Federal Housing Administration has reduced the interest rate on home mortgages by providing insurance to the lender and thus reducing the risks. The Rural Electrification Administration was set up to make loans for rural electric lines at low rates of interest.

The Federal Government is not only the world's largest banker but also the largest insurance company, with its unemployment and old-age and veterans' insurance systems in addition to the insurance of many kinds of private lending for homes, small business ventures, and farms.

The question of the proper boundary between government enterprise and private enterprise continually arises in American political life. The Republicans generally dislike public enterprises where private ones can be used, for example in hydroelectric power projects. The Democrats under the New Deal experimented with public power projects such as those on the Tennessee and Columbia rivers, partly as direct competitors, or "yardsticks," to aid in the regulation of private power rates.

But neither Democrats nor Republicans have any leaning toward socialism as a principle of action. Neither party wants any enterprise to be run by the Government unless

Government and Business

there is some strong reason for preferring public operation. There are three main principles that ordinarily determine the choice between public and private enterprise.

First, if the public wants a service, such as flood control or weather prediction, and there is no convenient way to make the consumers pay for it, the government is asked to step in.

Second, if the public wants a service like common school education or old-age insurance that the government can provide more cheaply than private enterprise, the government will go into that line of work.

Third, if a natural monopoly, such as the postal system or the telephone, does not seem to be satisfactory as a regulated private utility, there will be demands for government ownership. The parcel post was created because of dissatisfaction with the express companies. Most of the water-supply systems and some of the electric-power systems in the United States have been taken over by municipal governments. The telephone companies constantly advertise the superiority of their service so as to ward off public dissatisfaction and the danger of nationalization. The American people prefer to have the natural monopolies or near-monopolies, such as railroad, telephone, telegraph, radio, and airline systems, operated by private concerns under government regulation. But the possibility of public ownership is there as a check against excessive arrogance or corruption of the regulating agencies.

These principles of distinction between the fields of government and of business are typical of the American attitudes in this highly complicated field of action. Most of the budgets of Federal, State, and local governments, including the defense program, are devoted to transactions that directly concern the business world. In all these millions of small and large relationships, the middle-class, free-enterprise, common-sense line of approach is the one that the American people try to take at all times. The political arguments are never about whether to abandon the middle way and try a fascist or communist system. The arguments are about the exact location of the middle.

XI.
INDIVIDUAL RIGHTS

IN THE WORDS OF THE DECLARATION OF INDEPENDENCE: "Man is endowed by his Creator with certain inalienable rights. Among these are life, liberty and the pursuit of happiness. To secure these rights, governments are instituted among men."

The Committee on Civil Rights, appointed by President Truman in 1946, named four classes of rights that it felt called upon to study in a search for better ways to secure these rights. The four classes were:

1) the right to safety and security of the person;
2) the right to citizenship and its privileges;
3) the right to freedom of conscience and its expression;
4) the right to equality of opportunity.

Rights may also be classified according to whether they protect the citizen against the government, or against other private citizens, or against common disasters ranging from unemployment to smallpox. This classification is most useful in a discussion of politics and government, because the three kinds of enemies that may attack life, liberty, or the pursuit of happiness are treated differently by the Government and have different political aspects.

Violations of right by the Federal, State, or local governments are treated by Constitutional safeguards, through the courts. The courts can order the release of a prisoner who has been illegally locked up, and the government practically never defies the court.

Violations of right, by one citizen doing harm to another, may be illegal under the common law or may be made illegal by the act of a lawmaking body. Many unpleasant kinds of behavior have never been made illegal, though they may be condemned by the churches or by

Individual Rights

other moral forces. Racial and religious discrimination often come under this head, and political controversy rages over the question of whether certain kinds of discrimination ought to be made punishable by law.

The citizen as a member of the community and of the nation has a right to some kinds of protection against common enemies, not only against invading bombers, but also against pestilence, fire, and flood. Under the old common law of England, he also has the right to public charity if he is in danger of starvation. The exact boundaries of the right to protection are the main subject of argument between conservatives and liberals. The Republican and Democratic parties differ on this point, and so do the wings of both parties.

When the American people came out of the Revolution with a new and independent country, their main interest was to secure their rights against injustice and oppression by their new governments. The other kinds of rights were well enough protected by custom and the common law to seem less urgent at the time than they have come to seem in later years.

The constitutional rights are now taken for granted in almost all the everyday relations between the American citizen and his governmental authorities. But around the border lines are always debatable cases in which the courts must decide how the right applies, if at all.

In 1951, for example, the Supreme Court held that the "third degree" was a violation of the Fifth and Fourteenth amendments, which prohibit the Government depriving any person of life, liberty, or property without due process of law. A police officer was held to have committed a Federal crime by officially using violence to get a confession from a person suspected of crime. Thus a new definition is added to an old right.

The Fourteenth Amendment says that no State shall deny any person the equal protection of the laws. A man convicted of murder was locked up, and the warden, acting under the prison rules, refused to let his appeal papers go through to the State Supreme Court. The Federal Supreme Court held that the State had denied this man the equal protection of the laws and ordered the State either to give him a suitable trial on his appeal or let him go.

The Fourth Amendment guarantees the people against unreasonable searches and seizures, and the courts therefore often have to decide what is unreasonable. In one case police had reason to think that a narcotics peddler had hidden some drugs in a friend's apartment. They entered without a search warrant and found the drugs. The Supreme Court declared that this action was a violation of the Constitution. However guilty the suspect may be, the law cannot afford to let the police catch him by unlawful means, or the rights of the innocent will be undermined.

The right to a fair trial has to be constantly redefined by the courts to weed out new kinds of violations or to forbid old and habitual violations that have begun to hurt the conscience of the public.

In the State of Florida two Negroes were indicted and convicted of rape by a grand jury and trial jury on which only white men were allowed to serve. The State Court upheld the verdict, but the Supreme Court unanimously reversed it because of the all-white juries. Another feature of this trial was that although the prosecution did not bring into court any confessions by the two men, there were reports in the newspapers that they had confessed. Two of the Supreme Court justices declared that this interference by the press was enough in itself to make the trial unfair.

The right of a defendant not to be tried in the newspapers before the jury has decided on its verdict has never been established in the United States, as it has been in Britain. In this Florida case we see signs of such a right beginning to take form.

Under the Fifth Amendment a witness may refuse to answer any question if the answer might lay him open to a criminal prosecution. But the principal leaders of the Communist party have been convicted of conspiracy to overthrow the Government by force and violence, and the Supreme Court has refused to declare the Smith Act of 1940, under which they were convicted, unconstitutional. Thus any person called before a Congressional investigating committee and asked about communist affiliations can refuse to answer on the ground that communist activity has been judged criminal and he might be charged with crime if he admitted any connection with it. The Supreme

Individual Rights

Court has also held that a witness can refuse to give any information, however harmless in itself, if it might form a link in a chain of evidence that would lead to prosecution.

The use of the Fifth Amendment may save a witness from becoming entangled in a criminal charge of Communist conspiracy. But it is no protection against loss of employment, since the employer naturally takes it to be an admission that the truth, if it were known, would be damaging.

Freedom of religion, guaranteed by the First Amendment, is still in need of redefinition from time to time. There are borderline cases of preachers who want to speak on street corners or in public parks, and who in some cases may be strange characters who are likely to start a riot. The city police have to decide where free religion leaves off and incitement to riot begins. Another difficulty with the border lines of religious freedom is that swindlers and racketeers may crawl under its protection by naming themselves some kind of church.

Freedom of the press is carried to great lengths in the United States, especially in the criticism, fair or unfair, of public officials. This freedom is regarded as a fundamental safeguard of democracy. But the legal freedom of the press does not provide as much economic freedom to print a newspaper as many people would like to see. Technology has developed in such a way that the larger journals can sell advertising at lower rates than their smaller rivals, so that in many communities only one newspaper can survive. The people have lost their freedom to read opposing arguments in their local papers.

The political machinery seems almost helpless to deal with this practical problem of press freedom. Occasionally a paper may be prosecuted under the antitrust laws for unfair methods of taking advertising away from a rival paper. But most of the monopoly is not a result of illegal acts; it is the end product of free competition. And nothing would be more improper than Government subsidy for the smaller papers. The solution of this problem, if there is any, seems to be not in any political action but in new technological developments favorable to small papers.

The partial loss of freedom of the press illustrates how a constitutional right may overlap the border line of an economic or social right which the Government may not be wholly able to guarantee. Other examples are found in many of the problems connected with racial and religious discrimination.

The American people have come from many nations. Those who came from northwestern Europe have merged to form the dominant group, which holds most of the property and most of the political power. The others are more apt to suffer discrimination when they are easily recognized as different, either by their religion and customs, or above all by their color. Negroes, Chinese, Japanese, Mexicans, American Indians, and Hispano-Americans descended from the first Spanish settlers in the Rio Grande Valley are all liable to discrimination in one way or another. So also are Jews and Catholics and members of some of the small Protestant churches such as Jehovah's Witnesses. Nearly all the people from eastern and southern Europe are liable to be treated as alien as long as they live together in large groups and speak their own languages.

A large part of the discrimination against minorities has been caused by fear of unemployment. Workers cling to any visible difference of race, religion, or national origin that can be used as an excuse for monopolizing the chance to get a job. The long period of high employment from 1940 on did much to relax this type of exclusiveness, even against Negroes.

The report of President Truman's Committee on Civil Rights listed a wide variety of injustices to which minority citizens were liable. The observation of injustices and recommendation of remedies was the special task for which the committee was appointed. But as a background for this enumeration of glaring evils, it pointed out that American life includes a high degree of freedom and opportunity, even for minorities, and that civil rights have been gaining more and more security from decade to decade.

Under the right to safety and security of the person, the committee reported a reduction of deaths by mob action from a high of more than a hundred and fifty per year in the first ten years of this century to a low of less than six per year after 1940. But in addition to the few who were killed in recent years, several times as many victims were rescued from mobs by local officials. The Tuskegee Institute, which maintains careful records of lynchings, has reported that in seven years before 1946, 226 persons were rescued from threatened lynching, over 200 being Negroes.

Mob violence is reduced by education and prosperity and by improvement in the character of sheriffs and police. In recent years many a sheriff who stood up against a mob has found that it would not overrun him.

President Truman recommended that Congress make lynching a Federal crime, but the bill was killed in the Senate by a filibuster.

Other violations of personal safety and security include police brutality and prejudiced treatment in the courts. These offenses are usually in violation of the Federal Constitution and can be handled by the U. S. Supreme Court. So also with the occasional case of "peonage" that comes to light. Peonage is possible only where the people are poor, intimidated, and ignorant of their rights; an unscrupulous person gets the victim in debt and makes him believe that he is bound to work until the debt is paid.

Citizenship is guaranteed to all persons born in the United States, whatever their ancestry. But many natives of Asia have been denied naturalization although their children were born citizens. In California and some other Western States, aliens not eligible to citizenship have been excluded from owning farms, and in some cases even from being supported on farms owned by their citizen children. In law the Federal Government has authority to correct such discriminations by making a treaty or changing the immigration laws, but in politics such action may not be possible until public opinion has developed a more tolerant attitude.

The right to vote has been restricted by many legal devices, which one by one have been declared unconstitutional. In some parts of the South, Negroes are kept from voting by fear of mob action, but the statistics of the 1952 election indicate an increasing Negro vote in most Southern communities.

In 1921 eleven Southern States required the payment of a poll tax as a condition of voting. This tax excluded poor people of both races; in 1944 it was reported that only about 10 per cent of the potential voters in the poll-tax States went to the polls. This is the last of the property qualifications which were universal a hundred and fifty years ago. Efforts to abolish the poll tax by Federal law have been resisted by filibuster in the Senate; but several States have repealed the tax on their own motion.

Another of the privileges of citizenship is the right to bear arms. This right, dangerous as it is, stands as a mark of the democratic goal of civil equality for minorities. In the armed forces Negroes and other minorities in the past have generally been assigned to noncombatant jobs or to segregated units. The officers' schools have seldom admitted Negroes. In recent years all the armed forces have been ordered to do away with racial discrimination as rapidly as possible.

Experience in France in 1945 indicated that when white soldiers are ordered to accept Negroes in their fighting units, many of them do not like the idea. But after seeing the Negroes fight, nearly all the white soldiers, including Southerners, like and respect them. By 1953 the "integration" of Negroes into units of the armed forces without regard to color had given such satisfactory results that it was progressing under its own steam. The complete abolition of the color line in the forces would appear to be possible.

This relaxation of prejudice occurs in many other situations when segregation is ended—when Negroes are admitted to white theaters or restaurants for instance. Experiments have shown that Negroes can often be brought into factories to work alongside white workers without any such violent resistance as is sometimes feared.

The fact that race prejudices often melt away instead of flaming into violence when segregation is abolished lends encouragement to those who want laws against segregation. They argue that compulsory abolition will be readily accepted in many situations where the present custom would not die away for a long time if left undisturbed.

In 1941 President Roosevelt set up a Fair Employment Practice Committee to promote equality of treatment in government jobs and in private industry working on war orders. This committee found that about four out of five cases that came up for its consideration concerned Negroes who were excluded from jobs or forced to take lower pay

Individual Rights

than white workers. Eight per cent of the complaints involved religious prejudice, most of it against Jews. Government agencies, business concerns, and labor unions were all guilty of unequal treatment toward minorities. During the war while President Roosevelt's Committee was operating the inequalities in job opportunities were considerably reduced, largely because of labor scarcity.

Several States have fair employment practice laws. In the States where such laws can be passed, public opinion is favorable to greater equality, and the law is often effective in persuading employers to hire minority workers. Attempts to pass a Federal law that would try to force equality in all the States have been blocked in the Senate.

In education and other public services many of the States require segregation of Negroes from whites. In 1896 the Supreme Court held that segregation laws did not violate the Fourteenth Amendment by denying Negroes the equal protection of the laws provided the State supplied "separate but equal" services. This decision was attacked by Justice Harlan at the time in a dissenting opinion.

The fact is that public schools and other services for Negroes have practically never been equal in physical equipment or quality of service to the similar provision for white people. Moreover, the fact of enforced separation, as Justice Harlan said, "puts the brand of servitude and degradation upon a large class of our fellow citizens, our equals before the law. The thin disguise of 'equal' accommodations . . . will not mislead anyone."

The decision of 1896 held for about forty years. Then the Court gradually began to point out the fact that services were not equal and in most cases could not be made equal while they remained segregated. The increasing strictness of the Court, the high cost of setting up first-class universities solely for Negroes, and a notable growth of tolerance in the South, especially among college students, led to the admission of Negro students into a few Southern colleges. The lack of violence or other untoward reactions to this innovation tends to cause it to spread.

Entirely outside the field of government, the action of several big-league professional baseball teams in taking on Negro players has helped to improve the position of the whole race. Baseball is a game that millions of Americans regard as almost a sacred symbol, like the flag or the Constitution, and one that comes much closer to their daily lives and interests. To be allowed to play in the World Series is a mark of recognition as a full-sized American citizen. The threatened rebellion of certain teams against the presence of a Negro on the Brooklyn Dodgers, and the terms in which the president of the league is reported to have dealt with the rebellious players both indicated that the recognition of equality was precisely the point. As the League President said, "This is the United States of America and one citizen has as much right to play as another."

The right of a citizen to be protected by the Government against all enemies, human or nonhuman, overlaps the right to equality of treatment at many points. In particular, when unemployment, ignorance, poverty, and disease attack the people, the minority groups always suffer more than the ruling majority. But all men are liable to disease and death, and the vast majority are liable to risks of unemployment or other losses of income. Great numbers of people work for wages and need some legal protection of their bargaining position if they are to enjoy what they regard as a fair standard of living.

The conditions of labor have been matters of concern to European and American governments for many centuries. In medieval times the government's interest was likely to take the form of protecting the upper classes against rebellious and disorderly workers. In the nineteenth century a favorite form of intervention was the suppression of labor unions, which under the common law were regarded as conspiracies. Today the laws have swung far toward the side of protecting the workers from arbitrary action of employers and from certain common types of misfortune.

The National Industrial Recovery Act of 1933 guaranteed to labor the right to organize and forced employers to recognize the unions as bargaining agents for the workers. The Wagner Act and the Taft-Hartley Act have further defined the rights of labor and employers, the first leaning toward the side of labor and the second swinging toward the employers' side. The public purpose of all these laws is to establish rules that can be enforced by the

Individual Rights

courts, to bring peace between employers and workers on a fair basis.

Where the politics comes in is in the fluctuating definition of fairness. The workers suffered oppression in the past. They had to fight for the right to organize, often with bloodshed. Their leaders were fighters more than negotiators. Then the law came to their side. Popular sympathy for the underdog gradually evaporated as the unions proved that they were no longer underdogs. Then the political tides brought the Republican party into control in Congress in 1947, and they passed the Taft-Hartley Act to protect the rights of employers. The labor-union members, in the meantime, are far from united in any determined struggle against either the "capitalists" or the Republican party. They helped to vote the Republicans into office in the election of 1952. The moral is that the rights of labor are well enough secured to leave the workers free to vote on many other issues.

The United States lagged behind most of the civilized world in adopting a national social security system, though many of the States had long had social security laws of one kind or another. Since the national law was passed in 1935, old age and survivors' insurance has been somewhat increased and extended to many more kinds of workers. Other features such as unemployment insurance, public assistance for the disabled and the blind, and aid to dependent children are gradually being extended by either the Federal Government or the States. The fact that social security helps to maintain the buying power of people in sickness or old age, and also in case of widespread unemployment, has come to be widely recognized. This recognition of economic benefits to business as well as to labor has helped to broaden the support of social security in both political parties.

The many forms of protection that the American people demand from their various levels of government arouse a characteristic type of political controversy. The conservatives declare that each proposed new service is socialistic and a waste of the taxpayers' money and that private enterprise could supply all that the public really needs. The liberals say that private enterprise is not supplying what is needed, and for various reasons will not do so, and that the proposed service will really save the taxpayers money by cutting down some form of loss or waste.

The rights of the matter of course differ with each particular case. The political arguments decide the point for the time being and bring it back for reconsideration if new conditions throw doubt on the previous decision. On the average, the movement is toward more government services to protect the people against dangers that, in their opinion, can be resisted by the power of government.

The American people, in joining the United Nations, assumed as one of the duties of membership an obligation to help the U.N. promote the rights and liberties of human beings in general. A special commission on which Mrs. Franklin D. Roosevelt sat as American representative and chairman drew up a Declaration of Human Rights which was adopted by the U.N. General Assembly, in the face of strong resistance by the Soviet Union and its satellites.

The Declaration of Human Rights goes considerably beyond the Bill of Rights in the American Constitution, simply because new forms of wrong have been brought into play by Hitler and the Soviet Union. Genocide, for instance, or the official action of a government to wipe out a whole race, tribe, or religious group, was an ancient crime revived by the totalitarians of the twentieth century, and therefore was given special attention in the United Nations.

In addition to the Declaration of Human Rights, the commission was directed to write a covenant in the form of a treaty which would be presented to the member nations for ratification. The original proposal would have included all classes of rights, not only for protection against oppression and injustice, but also for protection against misfortunes such as unemployment. The American position was that there should be two covenants. One would deal with obligations like those in our Bill of Rights, which could be enforced in a court. In the other would be obligations that governments would assume to struggle against evils such as poverty and disease, for which no absolute cure can be expected. The latter form of "right" cannot be enforced by going to court, but by political action to punish or reward the party in power according to the people's judgment of its success in protecting them from harm while

Individual Rights

maintaining a proper balance of public and private responsibility.

Neither of the covenants is likely to be presented to the United States Senate for ratification. The principal objection is that not all the rights now included in American law have been agreed upon by the other U.N. members for inclusion in the covenants. Although there is powerful legal authority for holding that no treaty can diminish the rights guaranteed to Americans by their own Constitution, this point is not universally accepted. The Senate shows no sign of being willing to take the risk.

The position of the United States in the United Nations, therefore, is that we favor the development and extension of legal protection for individual rights in all nations, but we do not expect absolute perfection anywhere. In our own country we see and admit many faults in both our laws and our customs, but we also see progress toward greater justice and equality. Our political processes are working out the principles of individual rights as fast as our understanding of them develops. We know of no better way.

XII.
THE AMERICAN PHILOSOPHY OF GOVERNMENT

ACCORDING TO THE CONSTITUTION THE UNITED STATES guarantees to every State "a republican form of government." There has seldom been an occasion to refer to this clause, because in this country arguments over political theory have usually been concerned with what kind of work the government could properly do. Extremists possibly hoping to set up a dictatorship have seldom gained even local power. In the 1840's, to be sure, there was a rebellion in the State of Rhode Island, and the President gave help to the side that he regarded as legitimate. In 1874, the advocates of woman suffrage tried unsuccessfully to make a constitutional case that a State government that refused women the vote was "not republican." In general the courts have refused to decide what is a republican form of government, saying that the question is "political."

The net effect is that the American people will decide by political discussion whether a government such as that controlled by Huey Long in Louisiana in the early 1930's is a dictatorship or not and whether the rest of the nation wants to step in. If the rest of the United States should ever decide that some State needed to be taken in hand, the situation might be called a breakdown of the republican form of government, and the Supreme Court would not object.

As a rule, however, the forms of government commonly regarded by Americans as "republican" are always maintained, however much their spirit may be violated by corrupt politicians. Every State government acts by authority of a constitution which the people can amend without violent revolution. The laws are made by representatives who are accountable to the people. All the individual rights that the people have thought worth placing under protection of the law are so protected in form, even if the enforcement

The American Philosophy of Government   119

of the law in practice is corrupted. There are courts where the citizen can appeal for protection against government oppression. These are the main features of what the American people call the republican *form* of government. They may not always work according to the book, but they are there.

In the twentieth century, as the people of the world have watched Hitler and the Soviet Union, the mere forms that the free peoples cherish have stood out as matters of supreme value. In a nation such as the U.S.S.R. the constitution may guarantee almost all the rights that an American would think necessary to protect his freedom, but if the people, in fact, have no means of organizing political opposition and challenging the officials who run the government, the guarantees are empty. All the forms of law that taken together make up the "republican form of government" are liable to corruption, but if the people have the right of political organization they can sweep out the corruption at will and restore their traditional freedoms. In a free country, if the law says that no one may threaten or watch a voter when he votes, and if the form of that law is generally respected, the people can choose their own legislature and president and require them to maintain whatever rights the people consider to be necessary.

When the people have the forms by which they can act as sovereign, their actions are determined by many conflicting interests and by their philosophy, or principles of judgment. The political philosophy of the American people is complicated and in some ways contradictory.

The American theory of government has been affected by the long history of English and American resistance to governmental oppression. The first notable act of resistance that has become a historic landmark was the struggle of the barons against King John in the year 1215 that resulted in the granting of Magna Carta, a written guarantee of the feudal laws of the time. Magna Carta dealt more with the rights of the barons than with those of the lower orders. But the people supported the barons against the king because of widespread distress which they blamed upon the king's extravagance and neglect of his duty to protect the people against corrupt and grasping officials.

A somewhat similar relation between lesser and greater

governmental powers occurred again in the American Revolution, when most of the people supported the Colonial governments against the king. Once more the people felt that the king's abuse of the law was the cause of their troubles, while the Colonial legislatures and their successors, the State governments, were regarded as champions of the people.

From Magna Carta on down to the Federal legislation guaranteeing the right of labor to collective bargaining, the ideas of freedom and equality that underlie the American tradition have been worked out, not by revolutionaries arising from the slums, but by people who were themselves privileged in one way or another. In the early days the common folk of England sometimes rose against their "betters," as in Wat Tyler's Rebellion in 1381, but their lack of wise and temperate leadership stood in the way of their getting the reforms they needed. Progress toward a more democratic society, as a rule, came by the efforts of men with power and influence resisting the rule of other powerful men and governments. As a result of this history the American philosophy is strongly "middle class." Organized workers, for example, seldom show any sign of thinking of themselves as "proletariat." They support their unions, but not as the instruments for bringing in a communist dictatorship. They use the unions to protect and extend their hold on a middle-class standard of living and to win for themselves the kind of respect that goes with a middle-class position in American society.

The American political tradition, therefore, comes down through a long series of conflicts between organized and respectable interests. The American Revolution was typical in this respect. On the king's side were the powerful merchants and manufacturers of England, who wanted no competition from the Americans. Their interests were organized under the legal authority of king and parliament. On the American side were American merchants, tobacco planters, and landowners, together with such of the workers and farmers as they could persuade to feel themselves injured by the British trade restrictions and taxes. The Americans were organized under their States and in a loose way in the Continental Congress. The influential Americans who supported the king were afterward driven out. Those

The American Philosophy of Government 121

who were left to found the new nation and write its history were strongly impressed with the idea that a central government is likely to be tyrannical, while a local government is good as an organized means for resisting the central government. In this they resembled their remote ancestors who took the side of the barons against King John.

This fear and dislike of the central government was the first principle of the followers of Thomas Jefferson. The motto of Jeffersonian democracy was "that government is best that governs least."

On the other hand, although a central government may sometimes encroach on the rights of the people and the local governments may have to resist these encroachments, the people have some needs that only a central government can meet. Soon after the Revolution, the country was faced with a condition that outweighed the theory of opposition to the central government. The collapse of trade and the weakness of the country's defenses were most evident to businessmen, financiers, and men in public office. Their leader was Alexander Hamilton. The Hamiltonians, or Federalists, although they had been strongly opposed to the central government of England, came out in favor of a strong central government in the United States for compelling practical reasons. Even Jefferson reluctantly went along with the idea of the Constitution when it came up for ratification.

The Americans down to the present day have jumped back and forth between the doctrines of Hamilton and those of Jefferson according to which doctrine each one thought most advantageous to the political purposes he might have in mind.

The most spectacular example of this alternation has been the Democratic policies of 1933–1953. Mr. Roosevelt and Mr. Truman added greatly to the strength and the work of the Federal Government, a truly Hamiltonian line of policy, although the Democratic party is descended from Jefferson and still professes many of his beliefs. The reason for this curiously twisted heritage was simply that the shoe was on the other foot. In 1933 the people were suffering a severe depression, like the hard times of 1786–1787 on a larger scale. The Democrats thought that the needs of the people could best be met by using the Federal power, just as Hamilton had thought in 1787. Theory then had to be twisted to square with the facts.

Along with the Jeffersonian and Hamiltonian attitudes toward government, the American political philosophy has been influenced by more abstract theories as to the nature and purposes of government in general. There are four principal theories of this kind that can be distinguished for purposes of the present discussion. Between the two extreme theories of anarchism and socialism are the two moderate lines of belief that underlie most of the political-economic controversies among Americans. One of these is often called individualism. The other has no definite name in the American language, but the essence of it is the idea that the Government ought to help in promoting prosperity. It may be called "interventionism."

Anarchism and socialism have had comparatively little influence on American politics. Anarchism is the extreme doctrine that the state is altogether a tyrant and ought to be abolished. Socialism, at the opposite extreme, asserts that private ownership of business and industry is the tyrant that grinds the faces of the people and that the State ought to own and operate all business and industry big enough to employ any wage earners. These doctrines have not appealed to the American people. The middle-class attitude of most Americans is unfavorable to extremist and oversimple theories. Probably the long history of swinging between Hamilton and Jefferson has also trained the average American to feel safest somewhere near the middle of any theoretical argument. At any rate, the two theories of the proper uses of government that are constantly quoted in political controversy are the individualist corresponding closely to the Jeffersonian attitude, and the "interventionist," which first appeared in American politics under the auspices of Hamilton.

According to the individualist theory, the only proper purpose of government is to keep order at home and defend the nation against attacks from abroad. This theory is also called "laissez faire"—"let people make their own way." It is based on the belief that people, other than criminals, will work out their own salvation in the best possible way if they are left to follow their own self-interest. They will co-operate, or compete, or resist their opponents, as their own

The American Philosophy of Government 123

good judgment may direct. The theory asserts that an "invisible hand" guiding the affairs of men into their logical balance will usually bring about a just division of the good things and the hardships. The few accidental cases of unmerited distress can be cared for by private charity.

According to the individualist theory, if anything goes wrong, such as the bankruptcy of a mill that supplies the only source of income in a community, it is the just operation of economic law. If the country falls into depression, that also is the working out of economic law. Any attempt to interfere with the natural process is thought to be dangerous and senseless; the fear is that meddling with the laws of nature may make matters worse. All these arguments were constantly used in political controversy during the Great Depression that started in 1929.

The alternative theory has no established name for the apparent reason that it is always on the defensive. Americans are taught to feel ashamed of accepting help from the Government; and they do not readily admit to having any general theory of justification for such help. So despite the fact that practically all Americans believe "there ought to be a law" when they think of something they want the Government to do for them—still, when they think of paying taxes to help someone else, they are apt to feel that such tendencies may endanger the American tradition.

The essence of the "interventionist" theory is that there are some needs beyond police and military protection that can be met only by the Government. The Constitution would not have been written except for the desperation of businessmen who needed over-all controls of trade to release them from crippling trade barriers and wild fluctuations of money. The Constitution was produced for the special purpose of giving the central authority more power to control trade, money, the postal system, and the patent office, and broadly to provide for the "general welfare."

Thus the Federalists, who were the ancestors of the present-day Republicans, started their history as the party that wanted the Government to go far beyond policing the nation and warding off foreign enemies. Within the limits of what they thought needful for prosperity and progress, they were all for Government help to business.

The same principles that led the Federalists to support

the Constitution led their successors to support protective tariffs to encourage the growth of industry. In the early part of the country's history most of the welfare operations of the Federal Government were of more direct benefit to business than to the workers and small farmers; the Jeffersonians were therefore opposed to expansion of Government services, and they clung to the individualistic theory. Andrew Jackson, who came to the White House in 1828 as the spokesman of the frontiersmen, fought the National Bank because its effect was more favorable to the city businessmen than to the small farmers and traders of the frontier.

Thus the principle of recognizing which side of the bread has the butter is an essential element in understanding why now one party and now another takes the side of individualism or the side of the expanding public services. But why should not both parties compromise by letting the Government give everyone whatever he wants? To an extent they do. Each congressman wants the Government to build a post office or a river dike in his district, and he will vote for other public works if the other congressmen will vote for his. There are limits on this kind of trading, commonly called "pork barrel," as a motive for expanding the work of the Federal Government. One is the public dislike of high taxes. Another is that many public services include some kind of regulation or interference with powerful private interests. For example, the enforcement of antitrust laws, while it may help business in general, is sure to hurt some corporations, often those with great power and influence. The victims naturally argue for individualism and for strict limitations on Federal activity.

Although the actual party arguments are usually based on special interests, they must not be taken to lack all logic or sense. The American people have found economic progress and escape from many threatened disasters in a two-sided political theory that lies between anarchy on one side and socialism on the other. They stay on this middle road by constantly arguing over the advantages of government help on one hand and the danger of stifling individual initiative on the other. Logically both these arguments are partly correct, and when the voters strike a successful bal-

The American Philosophy of Government   125

ance between them they get the kind of government the American people want.

The twisted inheritance by which the descendants of the Federalists came to be the champions of individualism while the followers of Thomas Jefferson found themselves expanding the functions of government, was largely the result of science and invention.

In 1800 the vast majority of Americans were farmers, and there were few services the Government could offer them. The Government bought or conquered the West for them and turned them loose in it, with some military protection against the Indian tribes. After that the pioneers had to make their own way. When they got ready to organize themselves into communities, they were governed by the natural leaders whom they chose themselves, and hanged their own horse thieves by their own efforts. This was probably much closer to the formation of government by "social compact" than anything ever done by a primitive tribe; for the pioneers knew in advance what the American forms of government would be, and whenever they needed these forms they held a meeting and agreed to create them.

Such experiences led not only the pioneers of the West, but the American people generally, to believe that small local governments were quite enough to deal with most practical problems, if any government attention was needed at all.

Then came the gradually increasing effects of science. The great transcontinental railways went through to the Pacific coast, and the people of California began to complain of exorbitant charges and unfair discrimination. The railroads were too powerful to be controlled by any State government. Then petroleum was developed, and the people shifted from candles and whale oil to "rock-oil" lamps. The petroleum business soon developed into a monopoly, and the people were not pleased with the effect. The people called for Federal regulation of railroads and Federal suppression of monopoly.

In the twentieth century the new developments came faster and faster. Some of them created enterprises that crossed State lines and had to be regulated by a power greater than any State. Radio could not operate profitably in the United States without some authority to allocate the channels. Air transport requires a Federal authority to oversee the safety rules and allocate licenses for the routes where a monopoly may be necessary. Each new invention that can be used only with some element of Federal management or subsidy adds a new bureau to the bureaucracy in Washington. Even the automobile, a personal vehicle driven by its owner, demands a highway system on so vast a scale that the States cannot supply it to the satisfaction of the public without Federal aid.

Meanwhile the natural sciences have discovered many possible services that will be profitable to the people—provided the Federal Government will supply them at little or no cost to those who use them. First came the developments of scientific agriculture and the Department of Agriculture with its pamphlets and its system of county agents in partnership with the States. The growth and spread of agriculture knowledge has released most of the farm population for other lines of work—one of the main causes of the high industrial production in the United States. The few millions of farmers who remain are turning out more crops than ever—so much so that the marketing of their produce is also a problem that the Federal Government has had thrust upon it.

The discoveries in public health that have greatly increased the average length of life have done more than merely throw new duties on private doctors and on local governments responsible for clean water supplies and sanitation. They have also added new opportunities that can be exploited only on a nationwide scale, and the Public Health Service of the United States has grown accordingly. Another effect of medical science and of the migration from farms to cities has been the need for an old-age pension system on an increasing scale, and one that will follow the citizen if he moves from State to State.

It is sufficient to mention other services such as the Weather Bureau, the Bureau of Standards, and the Census, and the many statistical services covering such matters as crop reports and manufacturing. These services were demanded as necessary auxiliaries for the complicated processes by which the American people make use of their science and technical skills. Many other such services are provided by private enterprise and others by local and State

The American Philosophy of Government 127

governments. But some can be economically supplied only by a Federal agency.

Finally, the most spectacular growth of the Federal Government was set off by the Great Depression when Mr. Roosevelt was elected in 1932. The people had had enough of the depression. They had tried the laissez-faire system of waiting for "confidence" to return by some natural process. They had tried to relieve unemployment by private charity and by local and State relief. Finally they tried using the Federal Government. Many of Mr. Roosevelt's efforts were experimental, but the people approved most of them as they began to feel the gradual return of prosperity. The seal of approval was put upon the general theory of government service by the Employment Act of 1946, in which Congress recognized the Government's responsibility to "use all practicable means" to prevent depressions.

This recognition, however, does not end the argument. The American people still favor individual enterprise and private business competition. Both parties have accepted many of the public services that were sources of dispute in the past; but the people do not want the Government to carry on any enterprise that seems unnecessary or that can be as well performed by private business. In 1952 the people elected General Eisenhower on a platform of "economy," which meant that he was directed to comb over the Government and cut out the deadwood and whatever services the people were not prepared to defend from the ax.

While Alexander Hamilton was leading the movement for an expanding Federal Government, the people who would be most directly helped were businessmen. They therefore were on Hamilton's side. When Franklin D. Roosevelt was expanding the Government about a hundred and fifty years later, those who were most directly helped were the unemployed and they therefore supported Roosevelt. The businessmen benefited in the end, but they had to pay the taxes, and a tax bill in the hand gives more pain than a rising income next year gives pleasure. They had also learned that government regulation of public utilities was unavoidable, and that they could deal more easily with State than with Federal controls. This knowledge influenced those who had public utility interests to oppose federalism and to favor states' rights. Thus the changes of circumstance, brought on by science and invention, transformed the Democrats into Hamiltonians and the Republicans into Jeffersonians.

But at heart nearly all Americans have one foot in each camp. We accept the necessity of a big Federal Government with reluctance. In theory we would rather see the work of the Federal Government turned over to the States, and so far as possible to the local governments. And we would rather see the work of all three turned over to private enterprise if that were possible. In 1952 the campaign speeches of both General Eisenhower and Governor Stevenson came back again and again to the wish for a reduction of the size of the Federal Government.

As for the hope of making any progress toward decentralization and reduction of government, the American people have no well-established theory of action. All they ordinarily do is to demand "economy," and then rally to the defense of the government services that they find necessary in their business. There is, however, a theory of decentralization that has taken root and may in time gain wider recognition. Mr. Frederic Delano, who was chairman of the National Resources Board under President Roosevelt, called it "unplanning," and it was perhaps best illustrated by the Tennessee Valley Authority.

The main virtue of the T.V.A. from its beginning was that it took over only the management of the river, the assurance of low-cost electricity, and some research that no one else was prepared to undertake. From there on, it was glad to point out opportunities and supply information by which the States of the Tennessee Valley, the counties and cities, and the businessmen and farmers might do their own planning. Unplanning means doing the necessary Federal construction, regulation, subsidy, or scientific research in such a way as to keep as little as possible of the work in Federal hands. The aim of a good job of unplanning is to create a situation that will make it unnecessary for the central authority to concern itself with local and numerous details.

The same theory of decentralization appears in an expression that has become common since the end of World War II, that the job of the Federal Government is to create a "climate" in which business will prosper. This is in no way a retreat to raw or "rugged" individualism. It accepts the Government's responsibility for taking all practicable means to keep the wheels turning. But the Government need not station a civil servant alongside every wheel to boost it if it starts to slow down. Better have a competent staff of experts who can recognize unfavorable changes in the business climate and can direct the considerable powers of the Government toward air conditioning the economic system, so far as that may be possible.

Much of the work of students of political economics since World War II has been concerned with the use of governmental powers to unplan the American system, to provide it with over-all air conditioning, and to release the private and spontaneous creative abilities of the American people. It is to be expected that as the methods for thus utilizing the Federal power are worked out and tested under the strains of inflation and deflation, the American people will once more adjust their theories of government to suit what they find to be the facts of American life.

XIII.
FOREIGN RELATIONS

Many of the peculiarities of American foreign policy have resulted from historical experiences somewhat different from the experiences of most of the world's peoples.

First of all is the fact that all the people of the United States except the American Indians are of "immigrant stock." They or their ancestors migrated to North America within the past four centuries, and they cannot entirely forget who they are and where they originated. The vast majority came from Europe, and in time of international stress they still love and hate the "old country" which they have disowned.

The forces that drove the Europeans across the sea included a strong infusion of fear and hate toward the political oppression, the hopeless poverty, or the religious persecution that these immigrants had suffered in their homelands. Their hearts were torn between homesickness and resentment. The force of resentment was boosted by memories of the long and bitter conflict with England from the beginning of the Revolution to the end of the War of 1812. So it was that all through American history one of the elements in the tradition has been a feeling that "we got away from Europe and we won't be dragged back."

At the same time, "blood is thicker than water." Most of the laws and customs, the institutions and standards of judgment by which the American people live are part and parcel of western civilization. Europe is the motherland of that civilization and still makes up about half of it. When Europe is threatened with destruction, the Americans are afraid that the bell tolls also for them. These contradictory forces necessarily produce great political conflicts in the United States whenever Europe is in danger, as it has been during the twentieth century. Such conflicts are intensified and complicated by the fact that the British tradition, which lies back of nearly half the American people, is often at odds with other European traditions, especially the Irish and the German. These ancestral feelings have not entirely disappeared in the "melting pot" of American life.

The second most powerful influence on the American attitudes is of course the geographical isolation that until recently protected the United States. A French ambassador, M. Jules Jusserand, once pointed out that here was a fortunate country bounded on the north and south by weak neighbors and on the east and west by fish.

But in 1942 it was a shock to have German submarines swimming among the peaceful fish within sight of Cape Hatteras, and it has been a worse shock to realize that Chicago and Detroit are within bombing range of Siberia on the north. Here, too, is a conflict between the feelings established by centuries of protection and the sudden recognition of exposure. The age-old terrors of Europe that we thought we had escaped have suddenly come knocking at the American gates.

Not only were the American people brought up at a happy distance from the marching armies of Europe, they also enjoyed the benefit, during the early years of the Republic, of constant quarrels among the European powers, especially France, Britain, and Spain. After Napoleon, for example, had decided to take over the Louisiana territory and build it up as a dangerous neighbor to the west of the United States, he changed his mind and sold out to the Americans because he had to devote his strength to a war with the British. The fact that again and again in our early history European wars saved the young and weak United States from interference created a tradition in the American mind that wars in Europe were no danger to the United States, but rather a benefit. This tradition had to be cast aside when the United States was confronted in the twentieth century with the two world wars.

American thinking has been deeply affected by living for three hundred years in a vast continent with open spaces for new settlement. North America was almost empty when the first Europeans landed. After the Revolution, the tide of settlers poured through the Appalachian Mountains with more than two thousand miles of open country ahead of them. The long experience of the frontier has created habits of thought and an optimistic attitude toward material progress which do not always fit the facts of the present century.

Another influence has been the long history of trade by sea. The English Colonies along the East coast depended on the home country for manufactured goods, and in turn had tobacco and furs, lumber and grain to sell across the sea. Even between one colony and another, for many generations the sea lanes were important lines of communication, if not the only ones. The oldest and richest part of the United States, therefore, was of a seafaring habit that influenced the political ideas of the people. Even the Midwestern pioneers, shut off by the long rough mountain trails from easy trade with the coast cities, took to the Mississippi with their grain and traded with Europe by way of New Orleans.

During the nineteenth century the development of the interior called for large amounts of capital. Much of this capital came from British and Dutch investors. The American people became accustomed to foreign debts and to the effect of those debts on foreign trade. Foreigners could buy American cattle and wheat with the interest money which they received from their investments in this country. They did not have to sell their manufactures here in great quantities in order to pay their bills. Thus the American businessmen became accustomed to selling their goods in foreign markets and to keeping foreign goods out of the American market by means of a tariff wall. The fact that the trade did not balance never seemed to do any harm. This education, lasting over several generations, was a poor preparation for understanding the quite different conditions of the twentieth century.

Finally, the attitudes of the American people must be understood in the light of their democratic institutions and way of life. Whatever faults there are in American political behavior, a lack of open discussion is seldom one of them.

The foreigner who has had occasion to visit the United States at any time since it was founded has been able to hear a vast amount of contradictory opinion. The newspapers say what they please; members of Congress contradict the policies so carefully worked out and announced by the State Department. The most delicate negotiations with either allies or enemies are carried on, as it were, in a flimsy tent surrounded by a howling mob. The most dangerous military secret may suddenly come over the radio in a speech by someone who uses it to illustrate the kind of material that he fears some disloyal citizen may betray to our enemies.

Such indiscipline may seem to place the United States at a hopeless disadvantage in any contest with a secret and totalitarian power such as the Soviet Union. The habit of wild talk is so deeply ingrained that little can be done to control it. Some Americans comfort themselves with the thought that discussion, however wild, has certain moral advantages over a sullen secretiveness like that which has hung over the Soviets.

It may even help to convince other free peoples that Americans, changeable and undependable though they may be, are not plotting any secret moves to destroy world freedom.

For about a hundred years after the War of 1812 the American people gave their main attention to internal development. The Department of State was much neglected and Congress dominated such foreign policies as there were. By contrast with European countries, which were always deeply involved in diplomacy, the diplomatic service of the United States was notoriously amateurish and shabby. Only rich men could afford the cost of being ambassadors, and many of them had no qualifications for diplomacy except a record of generous contributions to the winning party. In times of crisis, however, the United States has been able to get the services of some highly competent men, from Benjamin Franklin's time down to the present day, to serve as ambassadors and as Secretary of State.

It is natural for the people of any country to be suspicious of their government's foreign office, made up as it is of men who habitually associate with foreigners. The American State Department is no exception. The nature of its work puts it at a disadvantage in public opinion. If it fails to get what the public wants in its negotiations with a foreign government, the political forces at work are not well understood by the people at home. There is room for suspicion that someone betrayed the interests of the United

States—a suspicion that may supply the best of material for political attack. If the State Department has to adopt a foreign policy that goes against the common beliefs of a century ago, there are sure to be many anxious people who are disturbed by such a violation of well-established principles. Thus the State Department easily becomes a whipping boy.

The complicated network of foreign trade, alliances, memberships in national bodies, and resistance to aggressors, built up since 1900, has changed the old pattern where the State Department was practically the only point of direct contact with foreign governments. Today nearly every agency in the United States Government is dealing with some aspect of American life that has a vital effect on foreign relations; many agencies deal directly with foreigners or foreign governments. In addition, local interests in this country often run head-on against foreign policies of world-wide importance. For example, the policy of "trade not aid" has been recognized as vital to American security by both Presidents Truman and Eisenhower. It is under fire from a host of businessmen, farmers, and labor representatives, each wanting a small bit of tariff protection, but one that will cause a big loss of American bargaining power abroad.

The State Department cannot pull together all these separate and often conflicting departments, agencies, and Congressional committees to make a strong and consistent foreign policy. Only the President can dominate the executive agencies and make such diverse organizations as the Department of Agriculture and the Department of Defense work to the same end. Some progress has been made in building up a White House staff by which the President can keep track of all the ropes that he alone can pull, but perfection is not to be expected.

Only the President can hope to lead Congress away from local interests when they interfere with foreign policy. The President can talk to the people. The State Department can give him some help with the detailed explanations of foreign problems if it has a strong and well-managed information staff. But in the end the President has to be the leader. Great Presidents have always rested on the support of the people.

Success in world affairs depends also on some degree of bipartisan support in Congress. There will always be some members of Congress who do not scruple to undermine the Government's position in world affairs for their own political profit; but the majority of both parties will support the nation against all enemies, as they have sworn to do when they took office. The system of leadership, through which the desire to unite both parties at the water's edge can be made effective, is not so organized that it will always work. It worked well when the Marshall Plan was under debate in the Eightieth Congress, thanks to the genius of Senator Vandenberg. In general, bipartisan foreign policy depends on a fortunate combination of unselfish leadership in Congress and presidential capacity to get along smoothly with opposition leaders.

A committee of the Woodrow Wilson Foundation has recommended a constitutional amendment giving the congressmen a term of four years. The committee points out that when the President is not running the voting is "thin" and special interests opposed to sound foreign policy are able to elect congressmen who would not get in when the voters are aroused by a presidential election. This committee also recommends that the President keep the Congress more fully informed of his long-range foreign policy so that short-term and short-sighted proposals can be more effectively combated.

The difficulty of finding any foreign policy that will not arouse violent opposition rests on two principal causes. One is the common occurrence of dilemmas; the other is the reversal of some of the most deeply revered American policies by the changes of the present century.

Dilemmas are sure to occur in dealing with any cunning and resourceful enemy, such as the Soviet Union. The enemy devotes his special attention to creating situations in which the United States must choose between evils. Korea, for instance, has been full of such dilemmas. Whatever choice is made can be attacked as a bad choice, probably inspired by traitors. Such attacks are part of the cost of having any foreign policy at all.

In the twentieth century the foreign relations of the United States have been subjected to severe political strains at home by the reversals of old well-established policies.

The United States has been forced, for example, to take a new look at its century-old policy of keeping out of entangling alliances, a policy bearing the revered name of Washington himself.

President Washington established a policy of neutrality between France and England in 1793, only a few years after the country had gained its independence with the help of an alliance with France. Washington's purpose was to gain time for the young United States to grow strong. He refused to let gratitude to France drag the United States into a clash between the giants of Europe. In his Farewell Address he told the American people that "the great rule of conduct for acts in regard to foreign nations, is, in extending our commercial relations, to have with them as little *political* connection as possible." He looked forward to the time "when we may defy material injury from external annoyance . . . when belligerent nations under the impossibility of making acquisitions upon us will not lightly hazard the giving us provocation; when we may choose peace or war, as our interest, guided by justice, shall counsel."

President Monroe stated in 1823: "Our policy in regard to Europe, which was adopted at an early stage of the wars that have so long agitated that quarter of the globe, nevertheless remains the same, which is, not to interfere in the internal concerns of any of its powers." This further declaration referred to the Greek war for independence, with which many Americans were deeply sympathetic. Whatever might go on in Europe, the American policy, upheld by the vast majority of the people, was to keep out of it.

This was the policy with which Woodrow Wilson entered upon the troubled period from 1914 to 1917 when he was trying to maintain American neutrality. But the Atlantic had shrunk, and one of the other fundamental American policies, the freedom of the seas, was under attack. The pressure of events drove Wilson to change his mind and to ask Congress in 1917 for war with Germany. Before he was through, he was vainly urging the Senate to approve joining the League of Nations, and more than half the American people were in favor of entangling the United States in the League.

But the tradition of isolationism was not dead. As World

War II came on, the American people were slow to admit that the Nazis were attacking not only their European neighbors, but all the free world. Isolationism was strong up until the attack on Pearl Harbor and the German and Italian declarations of war against the United States. It is still a powerful undercurrent in American politics.

The traditional dislike of Europe that underlies isolationist feeling does not apply in at all the same way to other parts of the world. It has been said that "all Americans are born with their faces pointing west." Isolationism has not meant keeping away from any country lying toward the west, even as far as China.

The second most important reversal of foreign policy that has roused political controversy is, of course, the reduction of high tariffs. Tariff reduction was pressed by the Democrats after they came to power in 1933, in accordance with their party tradition, which had always been opposed to the protective tariff. The party positions had been somewhat blurred by the growth of industry in the South and a tendency for Southern Democrats to favor protection for their own industries. But the tide of history was running against the high tariff.

In the First World War, the United States changed from a debtor to a creditor in world affairs. After that time, foreigners who wanted to buy American wheat or automobiles had to earn the necessary dollars by selling something to Americans. On top of that, if they were to pay interest on their debts, they had to sell still more and earn still more dollars. In short, if the debts were to be paid, and if American goods were to be sold abroad, Americans must import more than they export. Making more loans would put off the day, but in the end, a creditor nation has to run a surplus of imports or there will be trouble. So it has to lower its tariffs or there will be trouble.

But American industry had the high-tariff habit, and it had political influence. A dozen years after World War I the tariffs were higher than ever, and the trouble came. The war debts collapsed and the economic system of Western civilization also collapsed. American tariffs had a part in the responsibility for the Great Depression.

After World War II the war-debt problem was less serious, because the lend-lease system had transferred American arms to the Allies without asking for full payment. Then came large grants of American money for relief and reconstruction. So long as the United States would give away several thousand millions of dollars a year, trade did not have to balance. But in order to get along without giving aid, the United States would have to admit more foreign trade. Hence the trade-not-aid policy, which has been imposed by world conditions, but which offends the inherited beliefs of a large number of Americans. Foreign policy cannot be an easy matter when it rouses such emotions.

In addition to these reversals of policy that have shocked many Americans, several other traditional policies have changed or developed with somewhat less shock.

The Monroe Doctrine is one of these. Originally it grew out of a suggestion from the British Government that the two countries join to keep the Continental European powers from attacking the new and weak Latin-American republics. Neither Britain nor the United States wanted to see France and Spain and Russia building new empires in the Western Hemisphere. President Monroe decided not to become entangled with the British, who might some time have policies that the United States would not relish. So on December 2, 1823, he announced that the United States would consider any extension of the European holdings in the Americas as "dangerous to our peace and safety." The British Navy, which controlled the seas, was bound to back up the Monroe Doctrine in the interests of Britain.

So the matter stood for the rest of the century. After 1900, the collection of debts in Latin-American countries became an increasingly serious threat to the Monroe Doctrine. European creditors, using their armed forces to collect overdue debt payments along the Caribbean shores, might settle down and stay. President Theodore Roosevelt therefore announced the "Roosevelt corollary" to the Monroe Doctrine. European creditors were warned off and the United States took over as receiver, to collect customs, keep order, and suppress graft until the bankrupt countries were set on their feet.

Landing the marines in one country after another deeply offended the Latin Americans. The Roosevelt corollary was repudiated by President Herbert Hoover, who had

Foreign Relations

begun a new and friendly approach to Latin America by a good-will trip between his election in 1928 and his inauguration in 1929. The Good Neighbor Policy was continued under Presidents Franklin Roosevelt and Truman. The United States has accepted the obligation not to intervene in the internal affairs of other American States. In the Organization of American States the defense of the hemisphere is recognized as a duty resting on all the members.

This transformation of the Monroe Doctrine calls attention to a common dilemma in the defense of the free world. The free nations will not welcome United States Marines coming ashore to restore order. They want freedom to solve their internal problems their own way. At the same time, liberals in all parts of the free world are repelled by the sight of the United States giving support to nations with dictatorships in South America and elsewhere. The Communist party also makes this a point in its propaganda.

The American answer to this dilemma, maintained with few exceptions for more than a century, is that a homegrown dictator in a small country is less of a danger to the world than the conquest of that country by a foreign aggressor. The United States therefore prefers to help a country keep its independence even if it has not yet been able to set up a democratic government.

The traditional American doctrine of "freedom of the seas" was inherited from the British, who since the days of the first Queen Elizabeth have insisted on sailing and trading all over the world. That doctrine, however, has turned out to be unsuited to the co-operative defense of the free world against totalitarian aggressors. The right to trade, and especially the rights of neutral trade during wartime, came into conflict with modern conditions during World War I. President Wilson argued angrily with the British Government as well as with the Germans; but neither Britain nor Germany dared to allow American ships to trade with the other lest it lose the war. Finally the problem was evaded by the United States joining in the war.

In World War II, Congress abdicated American neutral rights by the Neutrality Acts, prohibiting Americans going into the war zones. That position also vanished as the United States more and more took the Allied side.

Finally, in the cold war since 1945, the United States

has led the world in demanding the restriction of trade with the Soviet countries. Circumstances have altered cases. But there is little political heat left in the freedom of the seas. Arguments are not about the principle but about what degree of control will give the best results.

Related to the freedom of the seas was the doctrine of the open door in China. The United States insisted on equal rights and privileges in the China trade. Since the Communist revolution in China, the question no longer exists.

Finally, it must be acknowledged that the foreign policy of the United States has passed through a stage of imperialism, which began to die out only after the Spanish War of 1898. During the nineteenth century the United States expanded westward to the Pacific Ocean and south to the Rio Grande. The most violent episode of this expansion was the Mexican War of 1846–1848. There were occasional movements in favor of annexing Cuba and other Caribbean territory, but they did not arouse any great imperialist drive.

In 1898 the Spanish war grew out of popular sympathy for the Cubans, who were revolting against Spanish rule, together with a fear that the Germans, who were encroaching on Spain, might come into possession of Cuba. The smoldering resentment in the United States was fanned into flame by a sensational press when the battleship *Maine* blew up in Havana Harbor. No one was more astonished than the American people to wake up after this war and find themselves in control of Cuba, Puerto Rico, and the Philippine Islands.

It was at this time that Rudyard Kipling in a poem addressed to the Americans urged them to "take up the white man's burden." There was a nationwide argument about imperialism while the country decided what to do with these new possessions. The tide turned away from imperialism. It is now clear to the vast majority of Americans that they do not want to rule any distant nation of people having different languages and customs. There is little political nourishment today in the old slogans about never hauling down the Stars and Stripes in a foreign land. When the Americans have to rule in a foreign country, such as Germany or Japan, what they want most is to get home.

The role of political parties in foreign affairs is not,

then, quite like their role in domestic matters. There is a general feeling for bipartisan co-operation, based on patriotism when dealing with foreign enemies or even friends. Only the most irresponsible demagogues are immune to this feeling. On the other hand, the honest differences of opinion on public spending lead to inevitable arguments over items such as foreign aid. Then there are the local and selfish economic interests that a congressman must view with due respect, or he may be replaced by someone who will. Finally there are the political effects of the great reversals of traditional policy, necessitated by the new world conditions. The state of the world is forcing the American people to learn new ways, and only by long and wide political controversy can they make up their minds and know what they are about.

XIV.
POLITICS AND DEMOCRACY

THE UNITED STATES IS ONE OF THE MOST HUMAN NATIONS on earth, as the Soviet Union is by all odds the most inhuman. Neither of the two great rivals is free of faults; but there is a contrast in the kinds of wrong they do. The contrast can be described in terms of economic organization, in terms of religion, or in terms of the official attitude toward minorities. One way to make clear the difference between the U.S.A. and the U.S.S.R. is in terms of politics.

The peoples of the Soviet Union are much given to political thought and action, if we can believe what their government says about them. Somewhere between four million and twenty million "political" prisoners have been reported as confined in forced labor camps. Justly or unjustly, these unfortunates were charged with political activities or with thinking about political questions. In the camps ordinary thieves and murderers are favored and are given charge over the political prisoners. The inhuman character of the Soviet governmental system is well illustrated by the fact that in the U.S.S.R. politics is the most severely punished of all crimes.

In the United States, just as in other democratic countries, politics as such is not considered a crime. Some politics may be a crime; for politics is human. It reaches all the moral levels from statesmanship to corruption.

Another distinction between the U.S.A. and the U.S.S.R. is in their attitudes toward civil rights. Both countries are made up of a great number of peoples with different habits, customs, and native languages. Many conflicts inevitably arise when such different kinds of people are brought under a single central government and into a single economic market. The U.S.A. and the U.S.S.R. deal with these unavoidable conflicts in quite different ways.

In the Soviet Union any nation or tribe that keeps its peculiar habits and customs—that will not or cannot melt into the dull mass of "Soviet man"—is liable to be condemned as useless and marked for liquidation. The central government will send its freight trains to carry these hapless victims away. Some will die in slave camps; some will be colonized on the shore of the Arctic Sea; some will be scattered and lost in the mass of the Russian people. As a people with a culture and a religion of their own they will be wiped off the face of the earth.

The kind of "natural selection" by which the favored tribes of the Soviet Union exterminate the less fortunate and survive to form the population of the future resembles closely the competition among races of animals, by which unsuccessful species are destroyed and the "fittest" survive. The fittest to survive in a police state are not the most civilized, but the most ruthless.

In the United States, also, there are many races, cultures, and religions, some of them so different that their members can never melt into the mass of the population in the foreseeable future. Here, too, there are conflicts in the markets and conflicts of race, culture, and religion, some of them deep-seated and bitter. No one can foresee the time when white and Negro, Jew and Gentile, Catholic and Protestant, will universally forget their suspicion and hostility and will work, eat, and play together without feeling any inequality. In the meantime many people hate and fear their neighbors who belong to a different race and creed. At times they take action to injure their fellow citizens. They may even succeed in passing laws to limit the opportunities of the hated minority. All this is human.

But friendship and good will between people of different races and religion are also human, and in the long run they have the advantage in a democratic society. The long run is long, and progress toward more harmonious relations is slow, but in the United States we see many signs of progress toward harmony and good will. This progress gives us confidence that the institutions and customs of the American way of life have some truth in them.

The American people do not authorize their Government to solve an awkward race problem by genocide—by simply murdering all the people of an unpopular group. Instead they search for the most practicable combination of education, law, and public discussion to guard and enlarge the rights of all citizens.

Communist propaganda, especially among the colored peoples of the world, makes much of the ill treatment of colored races in the United States. Americans cannot escape from this propaganda. We have to face it and meet it with evidence of improvement. Americans will not adopt the Soviet method—exterminating the minorities and hiding the crime behind a wall of secrecy. The American way is to work out the rights of the people by democratic means. The democratic way is slow but it is real.

The evidence that with all its faults the United States has some qualities that appeal to foreigners may be found in the fact that of the immigrants, who see the country's most seamy side, the majority decide to stay and make the United States their home. The freedom of the American people, imperfect as it is in many details, still covers numerous aspects of life, and it shows healthy signs of growth. This vitality of American freedom is related to the peculiar circumstances of its origin.

In the first place, most of the people who came to America had broken away from some situation in which they felt that they were imprisoned. They came to a new country where life was hard and dangerous. Many died of starvation and exposure and many were tomahawked by the Indians. But they felt that here was freedom; they had broken the bars.

In the second place, the Americans were endowed for nearly three centuries with geographical protection and opportunity that made freedom almost automatic. Behind them was the Atlantic. At all stages of the country's growth we could muster armies that were able to put up a fair defense against the forces that Britain or any other power could transport across three thousand miles of sea. This initial advantage was reinforced in the early nineteenth century by the good fortune of the young United States in the bitter quarrels among the European powers that prevented any one of them concentrating its forces against the American coast.

The other geographical element of freedom was the empty country to the west. There is much truth in the saying that freedom is the ability to go somewhere else. A powerful guarantee against oppression is the knowledge on all hands that the victim can pull up stakes and disappear. This freedom to get away is still a notable feature of American life. During the long period of the open frontier it was a dominant feature in the attitude of Americans toward authority and toward the rights of the individual.

Finally, the American people inherited the laws and institutions of England. These laws and institutions had been forged in a long struggle between the king and the people. They were designed to protect the citizen against the government. As the Fifth Amendment to the American Constitution says, the government shall not deprive any citizen of life, liberty, or property, without due process of law, or take his property for public use without just compensation.

These were middle-class institutions that the Americans inherited; and the distance from Europe and the open frontier helped to guide the Americans into middle-class ways of thinking. The American wage earner is more likely to want to buy a house of his own, or a piece of business property, than to regard himself as a member of the toiling masses struggling to confiscate the property of the capitalists. So many workers in the past have gone West and taken up land for a farm, or have started in business, that the idea of unchanging classes fighting a class war is not easily accepted.

Thus the laws and institutions of the American people have been well adapted to serve as political instruments for the defense of the people's liberties. As the automatic protection of the wide sea has shrunk and the free opportunity of the frontier has gradually closed, the instruments of government could be extended and shaped to provide new kinds of protection as the people felt the need.

Democracy in the first stages of American history was automatically created by the frontier, where any man who felt badly treated could escape and make his way according to his abilities. In the settled country along the East coast, however, the social and economic classes of England were established. Political democracy was limited to men of property, who alone had the right to vote.

But the frontier moved westward, and the plain men began to outvote the gentlemen. Political democracy spread as the voting privilege was granted to more and more classes of men and finally to women. The people took over the right to elect the President and the members of the Senate. As the political power passed out of the exclusive control of the upper classes, politics came to reflect more closely the common virtues and faults of the whole population. On these virtues and faults the United States in the crises of the twentieth century has to stand or fall.

The people are making their own decisions about what is right and what is wrong, what is wise and what is foolish. The common saying that the voice of the people is the voice of God can be taken to mean that in truth the instrument that is creating the American society is the voice of the people stating their sovereign will. When an obscure question can be answered only by experimenting with trial and error, the people experiment. By error they learn what is unwise, and by doing wrong they finally learn what is wrong. Sometimes the people do what is right and like the results.

The people seem to have done wrong after World War I when they refused to join in the League of Nations, when they retreated from responsibility for world security and instead played with vain promises of peace. How were they to know they were wrong? They knew by hard experience after their paper bulwarks against war were swept away at Pearl Harbor. The next time they knew better.

The next time, the American people eagerly joined in founding the United Nations and in helping it to survive and gain strength. It was the United States that led the way in meeting the challenge in Korea, when only a bold reply was able to save the United Nations from death. Even before Pearl Harbor it was the American people who authorized the lend-lease program, and after World War II they authorized the Marshall Plan. All these actions showed how the people had learned from past mistakes and how they were ready to try new devices to meet new dangers.

No doubt in the future the people will sometimes do wrong and sometimes do right, and if they survive they will have learned new things. Their minds point toward progress in the midst of danger, for their history has made them believe in progress. This also may be a mistake but at least it is the only road that might lead toward a better future.

Politics and Democracy   147

The American people not only have inherited the feeling of progress, but also have found themselves reluctantly forced to march in the lead. They are stationed on the frontier of history where unknown forces and unanswered questions attack them. Right or wrong they have to take all that comes.

It is natural and proper that the political forces in the United States should press not only forward but back. There is room not only for boldness but also for prudence along the frontier of history. Moreover, there is room not only to show courage for what must be done, but also to bring up all the fears that must not be left to fester beneath the surface. All hopes and fears must be aired and the decisions when they are taken must be firmly established. This the American political system does with a fair degree of success in the midst of all the wild and whirling melée of controversy.

The United States, facing the fearful tasks of world leadership, is fortunate in the mixture of populations that makes up the American people. The tangled hopes, fears, and beliefs of the races of men, their hatreds and suspicions, and their need for harmony are not unknown to the people of the United States. All these problems we have at home, not all reduced to a harmonious pattern of good will and co-operation, but reduced to a pattern of living together that does not explode into civil war. That, rather than a dream of Utopia, is what the world needs, and thanks to their own troubles at home the American people are not entirely ignorant of what it means.

There is no Utopia in the American dream. For three hundred years we have been on a journey. We have traveled far, and we see no end ahead. This is not a goal but a journey to which the people are committed. Taking the rough with the smooth, the people like the journey. It seems to lead generally to higher ground where the view is better than it was in the past.

As the French traveler de Toqueville remarked more than a century ago: "The structure of the American government would be ill-adapted to a people which has not been long accustomed to conduct its own affairs, or to one in which the science of politics has not descended to the humblest classes of society." The American people cannot recommend that countries just escaping from age-old absolutist systems should imitate the American system with all its peculiarities derived from the peculiar experiences of the American people. What the Americans can recommend is that others who have won political liberty set out on the journey of democratic progress using their own traditions and their own genius, in the faith that with all its troubles it is the best kind of journey for any people to undertake.

The people work out the paths of their journey in many different ways. They use what they can learn from science. They use the guidance of religious teaching. In the ordinary give and take of everyday life they work out the American way.

In their governmental organizations they use democratic ways of discussion, compromise, and agreement as well as they know how. That is, they use the arts of politics. As between dictatorships, where there can be no art of politics, and the noise and confusion of the democratic way, for better or for worse the Americans face the destiny of the twentieth century committed to the democratic way.

INDEX

A
Adams, John Quincy, 21, 22
Agencies in government, 53, 54
Aid, Federal, 89, 90
Amendments, 83
American Fed. of Labor, 31
American Legion, 32
American Political Science Association, 69
Anarchism, 122
Antislavery, 23
Articles of Confederation, 9, 11, 12
Attlee, Clement, 29
Attorney General, duties of, 79, 80

B
Ballot, secret, 42
Baseball, recognition of equality in, 114
Bentham, Jeremy, 80
Bill of Rights, 17, 116
Blackstone, Sir William, 80
Boundary, question of, 104
Bryan, William J., 101
Bryce, James, quoted, 10, 73
Bureau of Standards, 126
Burr, Aaron, 21

C
Cabinet, 50, 51
Calhoun, John C., 74
Cannon, "Uncle Joe," 65
Caucus, nominations by, 23
Centralization, 92, 97, 98
Checks and balances, principle of, 17
China, doctrine of open door in, 140; trade with, 140
Churchill, Winston, 29
Civil Aviation Board, 51
Civil Service, 52, 53; in government, 53; state, 89
Cleveland, Grover, 15
"Cloture" rule, 70
Committee on Civil Rights, 106, 110
Committee, National, duties of, 37
Committees, Senate and House, 67

Communists, 24, 25, 26
Conflict, in government, 62, 63
Congress, 33; defined, 56-58; duties of, 64, 71, 72; powers of, 16, 47-54, 64, 78; responsibility of, 58-59
"Connecticut Compromise," 13
Constitution, 9, 10, 11, 13, 14, 16, 18, 20; articles of, 17; when government violates, 73, 74
Continental Congress, 9, 13
Convention, National, how conducted, 34, 35, 36; Philadelphia, 12
Court of Appeals, 76, 77
Court of Chancery, 88
Court of Claims, 77
Court of Customs and Patent Appeals, 77
Court, composition of Supreme, 75; district, 76; duties of Federal, 73; inferior, 76; magistrates, 88; power of Federal, 74; powers of Supreme, 77, 107, 108, 117; state, 87, 88

D
Decentralization, theory of, 128-29
Declaration of Human Rights, 17, 116
Declaration of Independence, 9, 60, 106
Declaration of Rights and Grievances, 9
Delano, Frederic, 128
Democracy, meaning of, 28
Department of Agriculture, 98, 126, 134
Department of Defense, 134
Department of Justice, 79, 80
Discipline, lack of, in government, 60, 61
Discrimination, 110, 112

E
Eisenhower, Dwight D., 29, 60, 80, 91, 127, 128, 134
Election, national cost of 38, 39;

149

officials, 42; primary, 33
Electoral college, 15, 20, 21
Employers' Liability Act, 76
Employment Act of 1946, 127
"Equity" explained, 88
"Era of good feeling," 22
European Coal and Steel Community, 102
Export-Import Bank, 104

F
Fair Employment Practice Committee, 112
Farewell Address, 136
Farm Bureau Federation, 32
Farmer-Labor party, 30
Farmers Union, 32
FBI, Federal Bureau of Investigation, 79
Federal Communications Commission, 51, 78
Federal Housing Administration, 104
Federal Power Commission, 52, 78
Federal Trade Commission, 51, 52, 78, 79
Federalists, 21, 22, 27, 121, 123, 125
Fifth Amendment 108, 109, 145
Filibuster, in Senate, 70
Fourteenth Amendment, 83, 107, 108, 113
Franklin, Benjamin, 133
Freedom, 144, 145; of press, 109, 110; of religion, 109
"Freedom of the seas," 139, 140
Free-silver plank, 101

G
General Federation of Women's Clubs, 32
Genocide, 116, 143
Government, American philosophy of, 118-29; and business, 99-105; city, 93-96; county, 96, 97; commission form of, 94, 118-19; established during Colonial period, 7; local, 93-98; manager plan of, 94; mayor-and-council system of, 94; relation with business, 104; state, 89, 90, 91; town, 97

Governor of states, powers of, 83, 84
Great Depression, 96, 123, 127, 137
"Greenbacks," issuance of, 101

H
Habeas corpus, 17
Hamilton, Alexander, 20, 100, 121, 122, 127
Harlan, Justice, 113
Harrison, Benjamin, 16
Harrison, William Henry, 23
Hatch Act, 38
Holding Company Act of 1935, 103
Hoover Commission, 55
Hoover Dam, 13
Hoover, Herbert, 54, 62, 104, 138
House of Representatives, 13, 14, 15, 24, 57, 58
House Ways and Means Committee, 60

I
Imperialism, 140
Imports, 137
Individualist theory, 122, 123
Insurance, old-age, 104, 105, 115; survivors', 115; veterans', 104
"Integration," 112
Interior, development of, 132
Internal development, 133, 134
Internal Revenue Bureau, 79
Interstate Commerce Commission, 78
"Interventionist" theory, 123
Isolation, geographical, of United States, 131
Isolationism, 136-37

J
Jackson, Andrew, 22, 33, 73, 74, 124
Jefferson, Thomas, 21, 22 47, 121, 122, 125
Jeffersonians—"Republicans" 22, 27, 124, 128
John, King, 119, 121
Johnston, William Samuel, 13
Jusserand, M. Jules, 137

K
Kefauver, Senator Estes, 96

150

Korea, 49, 135, 146

L

La Follette, Robert, 29, 69
"Laissez faire," 122
Laws, 103, 107; fair employment practice, 113; social security, 87
League of Nations, 136, 146
League of Women Voters, 32
Legislative Reference Service, 69
Library of Congress, 69
Lincoln, Abraham, 23, 48, 73
Locke, John, 47
Long, Huey, 118
"Long ballot," 42, 43
Louisiana, purchase of, 22
Lynching, 111

M

"Machine," meaning of, 39, 40, 41; political, 39, 40, 41
Madison, James, 20, 49
Magna Carta, 119, 120
Maine, 140
Marshall, Chief Justice John, 74
Marshall Plan, 62, 69, 135, 146
Marx, Karl, 102
Mellett, Lowell, 59
Metals Reserve Agency, 104
Mexican War of 1846–1848, 140
Monopolies, 99-100
Monroe Doctrine, 138, 139
Monroe, James, 136, 138
Monroney, Senator Mike, 69
Morse, Senator Wayne, 61
Multiparty system, 24

N

Napoleon, 22, 47, 131
National Association of Manufacturers, 31
National Housing Agency, 55
National Industrial Recovery Act, 114
National Republicans, 22
National Resources Board, 128
NATO, 49, 71
Neutrality Acts, 139
New Deal, 69, 103
"New Jersey Plan," 12, 13

O

Office of Legislative Counsel, 68
One-party, States, 16; system, 19

Organization of American States, 139
Organizations, party, in Senate and House, 66, 67, 68

P

"Packing," 75
Parties, minor, 31; organization and operation of, 33-45
Pearl Harbor, 49, 137, 146
Pension, old-age, 126
"Peonage," 111
Philadephia Convention, 9, 10
Plank, meaning of, 35
Plunkitt, George W., 40
Policy, American, 136; trade-not-aid, 138
Politics and democracy, 142-48
Populists, 101
Presidents, of United States, duties of, 44; how nominated, 34, 35; powers of, 16, 46-52, 56, 58, 60, 61; relations with Congress, 49, 50
Progressive, Bull Moose party, 29, 30
Progressives, Wallace, 29
Public health, discoveries in, 126
Public Health Service, 126

R

Radio, 45, 125
"Recall" defined, 84
Reconstruction Finance Corporation, 104
Reed, Thomas B., 65
Regulatory agencies, 78
Relations, foreign, 130-41
Reorganization Act, 54, 55
"Republicans," 21
Revenue, sources of, 95, 96
Revolution, American, 120; French, 22
Revolutionary War, 11
Rights, individual, 106-17
"Roosevelt corollary," 138
Roosevelt, Franklin Delano, 22, 27, 49, 50, 103, 112, 121, 127, 128, 139
Roosevelt, Mrs. Franklin D., 116
Roosevelt, Theodore, 29, 48, 138
Rubber Reserve Company, 104
Rules Committee, 65, 66
Rural Electrification Adminis-

tration, 51, 104

S

Schuman Plan, 99
Science, effects of, 125, 126, 127, 128
Second Continental Congress, 9
Securities Act of 1933, 103
Securities and Exchange Act of 1934, 103
Securities and Exchange Commission, 78
Segregation, 112, 113; in California, 48
Senate, United States, 13, 14, 16; powers of, 57, 58
"Senatorial courtesy," custom of, 46
Seniority, in House, 65; in Senate, 64; system, 69, 70
"Shakedown" bills, 85
Sherman Antitrust Act, 101, 102
Short Ballot Organization, 43
Sixteenth Amendment, 75
Smith Act, 108
Social Security, 114-15
"South Carolina Exposition," 74
Spanish War of 1898, 140
Speaker of the House, how chosen, 18; powers of, 65
State Department, 132, 133, 134
State legislature, 84, 85, 86
States, Constitution regarding, 82, 83; rights and powers of, 82-92
Stevenson, Adlai, 91, 128
Suffrage, 14

T

Taft-Hartley Act, 114, 115
Tariffs, 137; reduction of, 137
Tax Court, 77
Taxes, during Colonial period, 8; poll, 111, 112; income, 75; property, 90; state income, 82, 90
Taylor, Zachary, 23
Technology, 109
Television, influence of, 35, 39, 45
Tennessee Valley, 128
Tocqueville, de, Alexis, 147

"Totalitarianism," 17
Township, establishment of, 98
Trade by sea, 132; foreign, 138
"Trade not aid," vital to American security, 134
Trading, 124
Tradition, American political, 120
Truman, Harry S., 15, 49, 52, 53, 55, 62, 67, 106, 110, 111, 121, 134, 139
Tuskegee Institute, 110
TVA, Tennesee Valley Authority, 128
Two-chambered legislature, tradition of, 57
Two-party system, 19, 21, 22, 24, 27, 28, 29, 30, 61, 95

U

United Nations, 12, 116, 117, 146
United Nations Assembly, 17, 116
U.S.S.R., 26, 116, 119, 133, 142, 143; politics in, 142
U. S. Steel, 80

V

Vandenberg, Senator Arthur, 62, 135
Veterans' Administration, 54
Veterans of Foreign Wars, 32
Vice-President of the United States, how chosen, 34, 64
Violations, of right, 106, 107; of personal safety, 111
"Virginia Plan," 12
Vote, to whom given, 14
Voting, 42, 43, 83; Negro, 14

W

Wagner Act, 114
War of 1861-1865, 74
War Shipping Administration, 55
Washington, George, 9, 21, 19-20, 47, 136
Wat Tyler's Rebellion, 120
Wilson, Woodrow, 30, 43, 48, 56, 136, 139
Woodrow Wilson Foundation, 135
Works Progress Administration, 51